A THING CALLED ASTON

An experiment in
Reflective Learning

A THING CALLED ASTON

An experiment in
Reflective Learning

by
NORMAN TODD
with Michael Allen, Laurie Green
and Donald Tytler

CHURCH HOUSE PUBLISHING
Church House, Great Smith Street, London SW1P 3NZ

ISBN 0 7151 2542 7

Published June 1987 for the Advisory Council for the
Church's Ministry by Church House Publishing.

Printed in England by The Ludo Press Ltd, London SW18 3DG

CONTENTS

FOREWORD

For ten years Aston has made a notable contribution to theological education and ministerial formation in this country. Its aims, methods, ethos, and achievements are still not as widely known as they deserve. This book both celebrates the Scheme's tenth anniversary and fills the gap in knowledge about it. It draws upon the first-hand memories and experience of those who planned it, started it, served it and studied on it. Both staff and students note mistakes and shortcomings. They and we can learn as much from the failures as from the successes, as much from the errors as from the achievements. However, the overall impression conveyed is that of a creative experiment which has resisted any tendency to be fossilised or institutionalised. It has already proved to be of immense service to the Church and of incalculable help to the education and growth of many ordinands: may it continue to flourish for as long as it is needed. Its positive insights and achievements need to be widely recognised, and I hope they will be gathered up in the continuing process and development of theological education.

ALEC NEWCASTLE:

1
WHAT WE ARE DOING

Initial Reaction

¶ When I heard of the suggestion that I should go on the Aston Training Scheme my first reaction was of horror, shock, disbelief and the feeling that somehow the selectors had arbitrarily picked the wrong person. I had assumed that Aston required one to read *Jane Eyre* and generally improve one's educational standard. I was on the wrong side of thirty and in a position of some authority in my profession as a microbiologist. I wrote a long letter to my Bishop . . .

¶ On hearing that I was recommended for Aston I cried with relief, such was the tension that was taken from me.

These quotations are from letters from former or present students. Aston exists for the students and therefore, in this celebration of our first ten years, it is the students who must speak first. All were invited to contribute their impressions, memories and more considered opinions of the Scheme. Many responded and we are grateful for their contributions. The responses have not been analysed so this is not a survey in any scientific sense. They are being used to give a series of snapshots of what it was like to find yourself 'on Aston'. Most of the initial reactions are of the two kinds described in extreme form in the quotations above.

The first one continues:

¶ I wrote a long letter to my Bishop who replied that I must do the scheme before proceeding any further towards ordination. Then I believe that God spoke to me through the prayer at the end of the Eucharist — 'through him we offer you our souls and bodies to be a living sacrifice. Send us out in the power of your Spirit to live and work to your praise and glory.' At that point I knew that if I believed I was truly called, and if I turned back I could never pray that prayer again. With reluctance I gave in and started the scheme. It was painful, challenging, and more than once — especially in the first year — I felt I could not go on. By now, four and a half years after leaving Aston, I am Vicar of two small parishes in Cornwall. Aston gave me a preparation

1

for ministry that I believe was as good as — if not better than — my subsequent College training.

During Aston I was enabled to increase my educational abilities and qualifications; but more than that I was able to gain an appreciation of the Church of England as a whole. It gave me a chance to assess myself with feedback from others whom I grew to love and trust. A painful two years — but a time when my personal growth was challenged and built upon.

The writer of this letter would have spent several years wondering whether he should offer himself for ordination; perhaps another two years in touch with his Diocesan Director of Ordinands (DDO); and then a wait until there was a place for him on a Bishops' Selection Conference. This would have been at one of the Diocesan Conference Centres where, for about three days, with fifteen other men and women he would have been assessed. The team of assessors consists of a chairman, four selectors, lay or ordained, each nominated by his or her Diocesan Bishop, and an ACCM Selection Secretary. At the Conference, within a routine of four interviews, three discussion groups, general chat and regular prayer and worship, the selectors would have been looking for pastoral and spiritual potential, educational ability, common sense and availability. Their deliberations would have continued long after the candidates had gone home, and eventually a decision would have been made about each candidate: Recommended for training, Not recommended, or Conditional recommendation. The conditions might vary but the one we are concerned with here is that the Aston Training Scheme be completed satisfactorily. These decisions are sent as recommendations to the Diocesan Bishop of each candidate. The Bishop is ultimately responsible for ordaining the candidate and he writes, usually personally, giving his decision which is nearly always that recommended by the Selection Conference. It is this Selection Conference which is referred to in some of the letters from students as ACCM because it is administered by the staff of the Advisory Council for the Church's Ministry, a council of General Synod.

The letter from the Bishop to the candidate would have been something like this:

Dear John,

I am delighted to tell you that the Selectors at your recent Selection Conference have recommended you for training and I endorse their recommendation.

The condition they make, with which I agree, is that you first complete the Aston Training Scheme to the satisfaction of the Assessors. Please make contact with the DDO as soon as possible, who along with the Aston Staff will help you to understand this more fully.

For the moment you should note that the Selectors identified possible areas of growth. These were:

a) your understanding of yourself in relation to your vocation and your experience of life.

b) understanding more of the breadth of the Church of England.

c) the need to acquire more skills to help with your theological study.

This might sound daunting so I want to assure you that the selectors found many positive qualities too!

With my best wishes and the assurance of my prayers.

Yours sincerely.

Hence the anxiety of the candidate, on receiving this eventual letter from his or her Bishop, and, in the case of all the people we are considering, being confronted by the condition of having to complete the Aston Scheme before going to Theological College and eventual ordination as deacon, or deaconess, or licensing as lay worker.

Here are some more of the initial responses to the letter from the Bishop.

¶ My over-riding emotions were of frustration and failure. I was frustrated that I had to put off going to college for two years and, as I thought, getting on with the real job of training for the ministry. I also felt that I had failed to convince those on my selection conference of the genuineness of my vocation. I now know that this is not true. By the time the anxiously awaited letter came from my bishop I had still barely registered what 'Aston' was. What struck me, on reading that Aston was to be my lot, was that in the Parks Department where I worked it happened to be the name on the litter bin that we used. Was this a sign? I thought. I should say that whilst it reflected some of my initial feelings, I subsequently became very grateful for the experience.

¶ There in black and white was just what I did not want to see. The joy of recommendation was tainted by a delay of two years doing a thing called Aston.

¶ I knew little about Aston—even of its existence—and could obtain little information in the diocese. My initial reaction was of anger and resentment. I thought I had to do Aston because ACCM felt I didn't fit the normal pattern of a C of E priest and that Aston was a means of fitting me to the mould. In fact the reverse happened as I discovered my true unique individuality. The fact that the ACCM report is not available to the candidate means that I didn't have a clue as to why the selectors did want me to do Aston. The initial feelings persisted until the Principal's first home visit which wasn't until the November after I started.

3

¶ My opening remarks to the Principal were, 'I don't want to do this and I'm only on this course because I have been told I must do it if I want to go to a proper Theological College.'

In contrast to these negative reactions, the Bishop's letter brought welcome encouragement to candidates unsure of their vocation or of their ability to cope with training.

¶ I never resented my recommendation for Aston, I was just grateful to have got through my Selection Conference relatively undeterred. While I enjoyed my two years on the scheme my wife and our two children were given time to adjust to my vocation while I adjusted to it.

¶ Although I knew nothing about Aston, I was pleased to be put on the scheme. I had gone to my selection conference with mixed feelings and slightly unsure of my calling. The Aston Scheme gave me a two year breathing space to explore my calling, whilst it was an encouraging green light as well.

¶ I welcomed ACCM's recommendation to begin my training with the Aston foundation course. Having trained as a Radio Electrician for my twelve years in the Royal Navy I had very little 'academic' experience under my belt. One of Aston's strengths, if not its primary one, is its flexibility, in that it can meet the needs of the individual without losing its overall identity. My own circumstances tested its flexibility. When I embarked on the scheme I lived on a houseboat on Hayling Island and was employed in electrical sub-contracting. I had three moves and finished the course living in Sutton Coldfield working with the Vietnamese refugees. The Aston staff were able to cope with me and support me through the upheavals of changing tutors, local churches and ever-changing schedules. My wife always felt she was very much involved in the Aston fellowship.

¶ I suppose I am one of those odd creatures who asked to do the Aston Scheme . . . I count myself very lucky to have been on it. Perhaps its effects are best summed up by a lecturer at College who said, 'You can tell those students who have been on Aston, they are clearly more confident.' That is what Aston did for me.

Although a majority of candidates have a negative reaction to being sent on the scheme almost every one of them finishes by being appreciative of the experience and some contrast it favourably with their time at Theological College, though others are clearly pleased to be going on to the 'real thing'.

The initial negative reaction seems to have been caused in the past by the considerable ignorance about the Aston Scheme among those concerned with nurturing vocation in the Church and by misconceptions about its aims among those who should have known better.

¶ My reaction to being recommended to the ATS was mixed. There was the relief and excitement that the selection conference was over and the way for training lay ahead. But alongside it was the feeling of disappointment at the delay. In the correspondence I had read concerning Aston the emphasis appeared to be placed on the lack of educational qualifications. The many other reasons why people were recommended did not at that time feature very highly, if at all, in the publicity material. However I was prepared to see what lay in store for me. Despite suggestions from my Vicar and others that we should appeal, I waited for a visit from the Principal. It was only after that visit that I became aware of other reasons for recommendation to Aston.

¶ I found that the rewards of Aston were dependent on the effort put in, but most certainly it was a preparation which enabled transition from full time employment to college to be made quite easily. Many of my fellow students at college were finding it hard to begin new courses of study, but the Aston students—and there were several of us at my college—found it very easy to settle in, having now only one thing to concentrate on, that of training instead of also having to earn a living.

A particularly clear statement of the transition from disappointment to appreciation is expressed in the following letter.

¶ I came to the Aston Training Scheme in September 1979 at the age of 36, and found myself to be the oldest student to have entered on Aston training at that time. I remember that when I heard from my Bishop that I had been recommended for Aston, my heart dropped—it was the last thing I wanted. A straight Yes or No would have been much easier to accept. I had at that time a responsible job with a Finance House and was under a fair amount of pressure to improve the performance of my branch in what was becoming a more and more competitive field. I certainly did not want the extra burden of part time training being thrust upon me.

Academically I had not achieved any qualifications, but felt that if God was calling me to full time ministry he would be far more interested in my spiritual life than he would be in my academic work. In short, then, I was to begin with both angry with the Church and reluctant about doing the Aston Scheme.

There was much unlearning to do before I was able to begin to appreciate more fully the opportunities available to me. Discovering 'who I was' was undoubtedly the catalyst of the many changes which occurred during my training, and continue to occur even now. The Aston Training Scheme Prayer is one that I continue to use, since I see it very much as a prayer for daily living. 'Building our lives on strong foundations . . . grow in understanding of ourselves . . . grow in understanding of God's world and the ministry to which we have been called.' These are the very things which Aston has enabled me to begin, and to continue now in my present ministry.

Aston was for me a mind expanding experience. One in which I came to realise that I was capable of doing much more with my life than I had ever thought possible. I left Aston in 1981 to go to Theological College full of expectations that the stretching I had experienced so far would continue. I was disappointed. The openness and questioning which I had come to expect and enjoy was replaced with a much more dogmatic approach which seemed to be more interested in proclaiming certainties than it was in learning to cope with doubts.

The Fellowship

Students all continued in full time employment, or unemployment, and continued living in their own homes. They frequently mention the fellowship they enjoyed on the scheme and a strong esprit de corps is evident. They were visited at home by the Principal, who seemed to his friends to live within the structures of British Rail, emerging with his motorbike at stations all over the country. The value of his first visit has already been mentioned by a student. The present staff continue this adaptation of the classical Anglican pastoral custom of visiting — though without the motorbike — so that their support and teaching is based on a personal friendship with the student in his or her home. From this base they encourage students to venture into the life of the course at residential weekends, the annual summer school and occasional regional get-togethers.

¶ As a whole part of ordination training Aston has made an excellent contribution. The fellowship is something which I have never experienced anywhere else. I only wish that Theological College had been the same. People cared for people, ministry was going on all the time. People were engaged from the beginning in ministry.

¶ With the Aston Scheme I made many friends with whom I can talk and discuss any subject. This has been rewarding, to share experiences and thoughts. It is very reassuring to talk with people who have similar problems, doubts and difficulties; you realise you are not alone.

¶ The weekend on suffering remains with me for ever. It's difficult to be objective about it in describing why, but I shall always be grateful to Aston for its Weekends and Summer Schools.

¶ I couldn't isolate any one single factor of Aston as the most important, for it seems to me that it has to be a complete experience and that omission of any one part dilutes the remainder. However, the 'Aston Weekend' has for me become of great value. Despite the amazing variety of churchmanship, experiences, cultures and professions, we all share the belief that we are called to God's service. To be able to share that belief, and to work it through with others who understand what you're saying, is a helpful and enjoyable undertaking. New friendships, fellowship and opportunities on the weekend are only limited by the impossibility of doing an infinite amount of things in a finite amount of time. The weekends are intense and hard work, but they have never failed to stimulate and challenge me. Opening yourself to new ideas, new understandings and new experiences is not, I have found, as painless as it first sounds. Aston doesn't shield you from these experiences but helps you cope with them and work through them until they have become enriching and useful. I find that Aston isn't so much saying 'This is how to tend the garden' as 'Look, here are some tools. Let's see what we can do with them.' The variety inherent in the 'Aston Experience' prevents you from making once for all blueprints. If you even attempt to suggest a generalised rule, round the corner comes the exception to it and hits you right in the face. Far from being confusing, however, this experience opens you to the reality of the world that we all so firmly believe we are to serve, and encourages you to learn from it. It is important, too, that my wife can be involved in Aston and she tells me it has helped her to see, and come to terms with, our expected future ministry. Sharing with others has given her the confidence to see what previously seemed vague and threatening as something full of opportunity and fulfilment.

An important aspect of the fellowship mentioned by many is the way in which, for the first time in their lives, they found themselves with people of very different traditions of churchmanship, expressing their faith in unfamiliar, and even feared, ways of worship. If this should seem strange, we must remember that many of the traditional Theological Colleges were founded, and are maintained, to justify and perpetuate one particular brand of churchmanship. The Theological Courses which prepare candidates for ordination on a part time basis, and which therefore draw them from a geographical catchment area, produce a mix of churchmanship more like the Aston students. Course students also appreciate having to come to terms with people who are respected as friends though of a churchmanship which in their former ignorance might have been anathema to them. The replies of students do not suggest that the result is a nondescript mixture of traditions, nor a settling for the lowest common denominator.

One Pastoral Tutor wrote: 'The outstanding memory of the scheme for my student will be of culture shock. He had never been near Anglo-Catholics in his life and he didn't even know he was an Evangelical.' And the students themselves wrote:

¶ The residential weekends were my first real experience of mixing and worshipping with others of very different traditions and backgrounds. This wasn't easy, but led to an appreciation of beliefs and practices which were previously unknown.

¶ I had spent some twenty-seven years of my life living and working in the same evangelical parish. As a result my churchmanship had a very narrow perspective. Only once had I attended a 'high church', and I hated the experience. Yet now, thanks to ATS, I have learned to love and respect much that is different from evangelicalism. Never once did ATS attempt to change my churchmanship, however. Rather, they helped me to discover the presence and reality of God in other traditions. From these widened horizons many friendships have developed across the full Anglican spectrum. For this I am very grateful.

¶ The major criticism I have to make is that the content of the course, especially the theological input, was totally unbalanced and unfair. If the Aston Course is to nurture men and women who are seeking God's will for their lives, it MUST give a full and clear theological teaching of ALL perspectives. This is not an evangelical's gripe at liberal theology. It's rather a plea for balanced teaching, for a charitable recognition of all positions taken within the Church of England and above all for a course that invites those training for ministry, who love their Lord, to enter into dialogue and discussion in openness, charity, and, above all with at least a basic understanding of others' positions. It is terribly sad to see Christians openly laughing and ridiculing another's position, like schoolboys teasing an unfortunate less mature peer! Sad to say it happened occasionally.

¶ One of the great joys of Aston came from the wide mix of Christians as far as tradition and churchmanship are concerned. Having come from quite a narrow background it was enriching to discover different modes of spirituality. At first many of us hid behind our labels and were afraid to open ourselves to others. As we learnt to share and mix, great benefits were reaped. Besides the broadening of my spiritual outlook, it helped me to find my place in the church. My basic convictions and beliefs are still dear to me, but I have moved spiritually and, hopefully, I am not as blinkered as I was. This broad mix was something I missed at Theological College.

P.S. I met my future husband on the Aston Scheme.

¶ It is here, in an atmosphere where each student is an individual and not bound by Church, party or background whence they came, that ideas and models of ministry can be explored, pulled about, transformed and even discovered.

At the risk of starting a mass panic, I'd like to suggest that *all* candidates for ministry should do Aston. With perhaps a year less at college. There are many reasons why I think this would be good, not least because I know of no college which encompasses the breadth of churchmanship which exists on Aston, nor the same sense of fellowship.

That this mixing was not without pain is suggested by the reference by one student to a 'bad Summer School when there was a lot of tension between the more evangelical minded and the more catholic minded'.

Learning and Personal Formation

¶ Admittedly there were times when the ATS was not appreciated. On one such occasion I remember wondering just who needed to learn most from the ATS experience, staff or students. In reality, however, everyone was learning all the time. Few, if any, of the staff would say they knew all the answers. Students were equally taught to recognise they did not have all the answers either. That kind of humility is, I believe, good preparation for all Christian ministry.

¶ The content of the Aston weekends was certainly useful to me in bringing out the 'I' inside 'me'. In one of the assessments I remember it being said that it could be seen that I was beginning to enjoy being myself, and was able to rely less on a function or label to justify my presence. That certainly is one of the things for which I am most thankful to Aston, because it is through discussions, study, assessments and social aspects that I was encouraged, being rather a shy person, out of my shell. One of the things I used to loathe, though, was the integration exercises which formed an integral part of every weekend and summer school. I used to refer to them as the 'party games' (talking to the person next to you about yourself/your journey/your hopes/etc. drawing charts of your spiritual journey through Aston, talk to the person next to you and then tell everyone what you have found out).

¶ Hated the OU; even more I hated the initial course on learning to read. Pathetic! Had a terrible phobia of exams, so OU made that worse. Nevertheless, I coped.

¶ I think it fair to say that at the end of three years at Theological College I felt very much that I had outgrown the ATS and had moved on academically, personally and spiritually — though I suspect that this is what the scheme is for.

¶ Not knowing what Aston was when I was told of ACCM's recommendation, it was hard to have any other reaction than that it was going to extend my training time. However the almost immediate contact from the Aston office and the soon to follow Open Day helped me to gain a positive attitude to this extension. We were encouraged not to feel second class ordinands despite the inevitable comments of 'when do you start your proper training' by those ignorant of Aston. This kind of reaction came from both lay and ordained people, but as a consequence of the course explanation at the open day I felt well enough equipped to handle such comments. I also welcomed the chance of the pre-course academic work since my previous study experience lay some twelve years in the past. I feel that my re-introduction to the world of study has been handled by those who are aware of the necessary tools, and though I have always been stretched I have at no time felt swamped. The New Dimension course was not only satisfying but also excellent preparation for the OU course to follow. The Arts Foundation course itself has illuminated a host of interests that previously were not even dimly perceived.

¶ I look back to my time on Aston as I approach my ordination in a few months time saying 'yes, it was worth it'. I value Aston's boldness in breaking from traditional theological education. My memories of being sent to see Aston Villa play Ipswich (our brief: to minister to the crowd), the Suffering weekend, relating King Lear to power in the Church, creating our ideal churches, continue to remind me to be ready to find the Kingdom anywhere – and they still excite me. No system is perfect, including all ministerial training, and there is plenty of scope for change. I value residential training, and long may it continue. Yet Aston's philosophy of teaching and learning being a continuous process suggests new concepts of training. For example, all ministers (including laity) should be involved in teaching and learning as they return to colleges for short periods throughout their lives. Theological training could then stem from, and lead back into, parish and sector work rather than being so much of the theological college as an institution. Astonians should shout louder about Aston because it is a sign of hope for the future.

¶ I received the news that I should do the Aston Scheme with thanksgiving. Coming from a background of limited education, I was aware that the only way forward in my vocation would be through Aston. What I did not realise was the fact that it offers far more than additional education and has enriched my faith and understanding of God even at this early stage.

Family and Work

Because Aston students continued to live at home the work had to be done within that context.

¶ The first months were difficult and a time of readjustment. Fitting Aston and OU with home and family as well as a full time job wasn't easy.

¶ I must say that over the past several months my family has been very understanding. It can be very difficult when you are married and have small children. At first I felt I had to go and shut myself away in order to study, and felt guilty at isolating myself in this way, especially when I could hear my children cry and ask 'Where's Dad?' Time is healing this problem, and the only cry I hear now is, 'Is Dad studying?' My wife, while I am studying, supplies me with constant cups of coffee. I can say as I have now been with Aston for several months that studying does become part of everyday family life and that if for some reason studying was removed from my daily life it would mean that I was losing what was not only doing me good but which also I am starting to enjoy.

¶ Being on Aston has given me the opportunity to explore my vocation to ministry in depth. Not only has Aston strengthened that vocation, it has enabled me to see my own strengths and weaknesses, and the gifts I shall be taking into the ministry. I don't think that, had I gone straight to college, I would have been able to explore it in this way. This exploration has not been done alone. It involves my wife, the place I work and the Aston students themselves. It is sharing with others the ups and downs of the course, the difficulties of finding time to complete the assignments, and above all the sharing of the corporate worship that brings unity to a disunited student body. In the rich diversity of our traditions I believe Aston enables and encourages us to explore our Faith through worship and discussion.

¶ Last year I was asked by a prospective Aston student what it was like. I replied, 'When you're on it it's hell! When you get to college you'll realise it wasn't so bad after all.' That remark was born out of my frustration with college at the time, but was also a genuine reflection on the Aston experience. It was tough. Shortly after starting I lost my job, and, without work for three months, became thoroughly demoralised. Consequently it took me a long time to settle into academic study (I'm not sure I ever did). On top of problems with work – or lack of it – I experienced personality problems with one of the staff. This was the result, largely, of genuine misunderstandings and lack of communication. Thankfully it was cleared up before I left. However, despite the problems, I look back on Aston with real gratitude. Through the pressure (and there was plenty of that), the suffering and the pain, I managed somehow to stay with it. I'm sure I also learnt more of practical use to future ministry on Aston than I did in my first two years at college.

The tremendous fellowship which existed is something that Julie and I have really missed at college. When we started she was welcomed to weekends, and the Summer Schools, as my fiancee. When we married it was good to be able to share the day with other members of Aston. For the rest of our time she greatly valued the welcome she received as my wife. She too feels she learnt much of value to our future ministry through the time she spent on Aston.

¶ I suppose I am one of those odd creatures who asked to do the Aston Scheme. Being unmarried I avoided a great deal of trauma that seems to affect a number of those on the scheme at the same time. Having no family meant that I had a great deal of freedom to adapt my life style as required.

¶ Bad memories usually consist of general weariness at having to travel on public transport to Aston weekends. This often meant taking leave on a Friday. With Summer School this meant most of my leave was used up.

¶ My initial enthusiasm for the scheme began to wane as time went on because of the pressure of trying to do a considerable amount of academic work, and carry on a full time job. If one took the studies seriously it meant that along with the residential weekends and summer schools a considerable amount of time was spent away from the family. This was made bearable by the excellent support system, particularly at the local level, and in fact it is probably fair to say that I grew academically, personally and spiritually, through the help both my wife and I received from our local contact.

¶ My main moan has been and will, I think, continue to be that the scheme is all right if you work 9 to 5 on Mondays to Fridays, or at least regular shifts with a flexibility over weekend working. My duties as a police officer on a city centre shift do not allow for this. None of the Aston weekends has so far fallen on my one weekend off a month, and my annual leave will not stretch to cover all the demands of Aston. (My Pastoral Tutor keeps telling me I should also take a holiday this year – the man is obviously deranged.) All told, continuously changing shift patterns, whilst notorious for doing nothing for your social life, equally do nothing for regular study. I long for the day when they, with the road menders when I am on nights, go away.

¶ The residential weekends are very thought-provoking and often demanding. It has been difficult at times to combine the weekends with my job, especially as it requires me to use my one weekend off each month for them. I am very lucky to have an understanding employer, who has worked with an Aston student before.

¶ It helped a great deal working for someone who was sympathetic to what I was doing. Not only could I fit some academic work into tea breaks and lunch-times; I was relieved of the need to compete with my colleagues. An agreement, totally informal, was reached whereby I would not be asked to undertake any further commitments – but then I had to accept that there would be no promotion. That eased the situation for me considerably, and to some extent at home as well. There still remained, however, early morning broadcasts and late night viewings to fit in, assignments to be completed, while attempting to learn where to put the bottle and how not to jab the safety pin into my finger.

¶ What did the experiences of Aston life do to me? Well, I gained a far greater understanding of myself, my family and self-inflicted pressure. It seems to me that it challenged and confronted the whole person, not just the academic part. The key thing was the availability of the team on the end of the telephone when they were needed, be it for advice or further challenges. Being in full time employment as well as training gave these experiences a grounding within society as a whole. The theory could be immediately put into practice as we developed our relationships both to God and our fellows. Yet being part time also creates the problem of being in two camps at once. The sense of belonging to a scheme of training yet still firmly rooted in day to day events of pre-training activities can be threatening.

Does this suggest a plea for making Aston a one year full time course? Quite the opposite! Despite the obvious difficulties of part time study, with the way Aston is organised the benefits outstrip the negatives. The sense of community among the students is not the poorer despite the often long distances between them. The sense of all doing the same course for similar reasons produces a feeling of togetherness. It seems to me that the Aston way is more akin to the reality of ministers being alone with God and their parish than the full time system where community and collectivity can sometimes give a false perspective of Christian service. The Aston preparation is invaluable for college. Those who manage to by-pass it lose out. The college system cannot prepare the ordinand in the same way. Aston has a lot to teach the colleges in respect to pastoral care and personal development.

Self-questioning and Vocation

¶ I learned to question everything I did in order to arrive at a correct order of priorities; nothing could be so sacred that it could not be a candidate for scrapping. However, I built a firm foundation of things which I decided I wanted to retain and build on. I had spent a lot of my Christian life working among teenagers, but had to leave this for the period of Aston and college. This rekindled my enthusiasm for the work which I am now doing again. Although college prepared me theologically I feel the Aston Scheme prepared me in the ability to get on with life one day at a time.

¶ While I still may not recognise all that Aston did for me, I can see that it did give me the first chance to ask where the root of my being was and to begin to ask what the grounds of my faith were in a way that I had not done before. If I were really honest I think I would value it more now than at any other time in my ministry. In preparing me for ordination Aston probably was the course that stopped me being a very foolish young man and enabled me to make decisions about my future that I would have been too blinkered to see before.

¶ Halfway through the scheme I left a social work career for a job with no prospects. Aston plus parish commitments forced this change. I had to hope for the best from the Aston assessors, and in myself I was better informed as to my calling and able to make a leap of faith.

¶ Aston opens the shutters to the student's real self, and the emphasis on self assessment enables the truth about one's real vocation to emerge, no matter how painful. It can be described as a wrestling match which involves an inner struggle producing many unexpected questions and situations, each tougher than the previous one. It enables each student to experience his true identity in Christian ministry. It breaks down the barriers of the stubborn heart and will, and establishes the facts like no other training can — the fiction about oneself melts away and personal ambition is destroyed. Every student is stretched to the limit, intellectually, emotionally, physically and spiritually, and faith is continually under pressure. Aston is not about achievement or success, and nobody passes or fails; it is about unravelling and re-interpreting, searching and developing.

¶ The great thing about Aston is that it helps to build the person, to give a good grounding. On these firm foundations which are often unseen we can gain a greater understanding of our call and of ourselves. By knowing ourselves better we come to our ministry far better prepared to lead and to minister to others in God's service.

The following letter from a woman student was published in the Aston Training Scheme Correspondence, a duplicated newsletter sent to all students.

¶ Dear Staff and 2nd year students, Having left the Aston Scheme for some time now, I thought it time to write, before the end of your second year, to let you know what has become of me. I praise God for his guidance, because I feel I am better suited to lay work than to professional ministry.

Six months ago I married my Dutch fiance and now live in Essex. The Church here is very rural and is nothing like I'm used to. There is one priest in charge of three old buildings and very divided congregations. Until my arrival the priest had no help — certainly the people do not believe in lay participation because, 'the vicar is paid to do everything!' I now do anything from visiting around the parish to leading services when the priest is away. I have also been set the task of re-educating the people and encouraging lay participation, unity between themselves and other denominations, fellowship and prayer groups. This has proved quite a challenge. I am thankful too that I am not restricted to the Anglican Church as I enjoy and learn from inter-denominational activities.

I am happy in my work and hope soon to embark on a Lay Readers Course, and also to become a Samaritan. For the time being I feel I am where God wants me to be. I would like to take the opportunity as I end this letter to wish you all every success and blessing as you finish Aston and go forward to your various callings. I often hold you in my thoughts and pray for God's guidance and strength as you move on. I am grateful to have been a small part of you once, and remember with gratitude my time with you.

A student who at a weekend had been describing some of his difficulties at work was asked to write about them and of his decision about his vocation.

¶ Upon joining the Police Force I hoped I would be joining a service of which the main function would be service to the community. In my seven years as a police officer that has been my main aim. I am able to derive a tremendous amount of job satisfaction, but only when I am helping others; when I feel I have the trust and confidence of a prisoner who realises that I'm not just another copper trying to gain promotion. I believe that the Spirit of the Lord has opened my eyes and enabled me to see what is really important in my job.

This student continued his lay ministry and chose not to continue preparation for ordination.

Conclusion

We finish, as we began, with two letters illustrating different reactions to Aston.

¶ I am afraid my recollections of my experience of the Aston Scheme are not all that pleasant, and I feel I was eventually ordained despite, rather than because of, it. I also have the dubious distinction of being the first 'drop-out'. I was one of the original 1977 group, starting in autumn, and was removed from it by my bishop the following February when he realised it was simply inappropriate for me, and that it would be better to spend two or three years teaching (I had just qualified) and then go to Theological College. The then Principal, however, thought otherwise, and told ACCM that I had 'withdrawn' from the scheme and looked forward to my rejoining at some time in the future. Of this I was unaware.

To cut a long story short, that statement from the Principal, combined with changes of bishops and DDO, meant that somehow I was lost, and it was not until 1982 that I finally started at Theological College. The Aston Scheme was then in its infancy and understandably did not want people leaving it so soon after its inception, so I feel there may have been a reluctance to admit that maybe, in at least one case, a mistake had been made. My background is working class: I was visited in my parents' council house, and I think I must have seemed a typical Aston candidate. However, I was also just completing my university degree in Religious Studies and Education. This, I suppose, didn't fit the stereotype and so was ignored, and I found myself compelled to start the course on, in effect, how to write an essay, before starting the OU foundation course from which there was no escape.

Looking back, I do not regret my five years as a schoolteacher prior to going to Theological College — quite the reverse, and I rejoice that God can bring good out of human failing, but *I do* hope that the Aston Scheme is now mature enough to admit that mistakes can occur, and that it attempts to deal with real people rather than artificial stereotypes.

And from a former student now ordained and just become a Pastoral Tutor to a new student:

¶ I took a fairly pragmatic view of being placed on the scheme. I knew my educational limitations at that time and I sensed that this and other circumstances prevented a straightforward entry to Theological College. My first view, then, was of mixed relief that the Church had not shut the door in my face, but had accepted my sense of calling and was able to provide a structure that could accommodate my training needs.

Looking back at the content of the scheme, I do sometimes wonder how everything managed to get done, for at the time I was employed by the LEA as a Youth and Community Worker. Time was at a premium, governed by the unpredictability of unsocial hours of work and the demands of home and Church life. What I feel that all of us who did the course can say is that Aston is no soft option, neither are students in any way inferior. I feel that many other students, and certainly those for Holy Orders, would have derived much benefit from being required to undertake similar methods of training. One of the key reasons why Aston is effective is the high priority given to the process of assessment. The student discovers the valuable training tool of looking critically at him/her self. The process is designed to enable self discovery as part of the very fabric of his/her theology. The development of self awareness, and in consequence a sensitivity to others, provides a foundation of attitudes necessary in Pastoral Care in the society and local setting to which the student ultimately finds him/her self called.

Memories of Aston Weekends, Summer Schools, are easily recalled. That awful Retreat House in Liverpool, the rooms cell-like and the beds so high and narrow that sleep was impossible because of the danger of concussion. A more serious and memorable weekend at London Colney led by the Bishop of Pontefract and Mother Frances Dominica on Spirituality. I remember the Summer Schools at Salisbury and Bognor, memories of deepening fellowship, the combination of hard work, stimulating lectures, the fun of having a 'Theological Butlin's' atmosphere culminating in the Leavers' Service. Aston worship was always an experience not to be missed and is still an inspiration when planning worship with others in the parish.

So I'm grateful to Aston, for friendships made, glad to have encountered men of God such as Bishop Mark, Robin Bennett and Bill Ind. They left me with much to bite and chew on, a vision of priesthood at its best and a model that I, through prayer, try to emulate.

Finally I'm back at Aston, not as a student, but delighted to be a Pastoral Tutor. It's good to be back in the Fellowship (did I ever really leave it?). I'm still learning from the scheme and gaining fresh stimulus for my own ministry, and I give thanks to God for Aston.

EXPLANATION

It may seem odd to have what amounts to the Introduction after the first chapter, but this book is not a straightforward history of Aston. It has come together in an order of its own, which expresses something of what students and staff call 'the Aston spirit'. The Governing Body decided that the book should be produced. One of the governors landed the job of producing it helped by the Chairman, the Bishop of Middleton, and the staff. This group of five (eventually six) extremely busy people planned how it could be made to happen. We decided to ask all the students and Pastoral Tutors, past and present, to contribute vignettes illustrating their experience of Aston.

A weekend conference for about twenty representative students and staff was planned and we set about producing as much as possible of the book for the members of the conference to react to. That draft was a strange mixture of letters, memories, documents, history, theory, complaints, financial analysis, admin. reports from outside people such as Open University tutors, and a long section dictated to an amanuensis during a car journey to visit students. Ideas for one chapter were presented verbally and produced a marked incomprehension and resistance. The last chapter did not exist at all. It was to be produced by the conference.

Even in its final form this is no smooth account. But neither was the emergence and growth of Aston a smooth process. It consisted of a mixture of aspirations, dreams, emotions, meetings, chance, misunderstandings, struggle, cussedness, dissatisfaction with previous training procedures, the legacy of charismatic pioneers and much plodding faithfulness. Even with hindsight and the inevitable halo effect of memory, enough of the roughness remains to remind those involved of what 'it was really like'. And we believe that enough remains for the reader to enter into something of that experience. The idea of printing the letters in Chapter 1 before this Explanation was to let them make their impact with a minimum of apologetic; to let them raise questions, raise emotions positive and negative, encourage sympathy and criticism; to allow you, the reader, to find links with your own experience; and, incidentally, to run the risk of your reading no further.

One of the Pastoral Tutors who is also responsible for prospective ordination candidates in his diocese was with a group of them in the cathedral explaining the Aston Scheme. Unknown to him an electrician was working out of sight behind one of the pillars, joining the multi-coloured wires of a thick electric cable. After he had finished the electrician came up to him and said that he had never heard anything so interesting about the Church. There is some similarity between the electrician making the right connections and the work of Aston, also making connections, adjusting resistance, investigating faults, in order that the current can flow through the intricate circuit. There is plenty of trial and error, some controlled experiment, some testing by results whether in organ music or effective ministry.

Because the book has come together in this way its literary form is rather like that of a mini-Bible, presenting the varied richness of an experience shared by a number of, and a succession of, people with a variety of involvement. It would almost be possible to do a typical piece of biblical research on this book, identifying its various sources and the way its oral tradition has developed and perhaps become distorted: the imaginary letter from a bishop, actual letters from various people, memories of founder members, accounts by the staff of what they were trying to do, reflection, opinion, interpretation, theory, description; and there are bound to be mistakes of one kind or another, and even some apparent contradictions as there are in the Bible. There are also some doublets, versions of the same events from more than one point of view, which can give a stereoscopic impression of depth. Here is a shared experience, something these people found exciting, challenging, rewarding and with a sense of direction. It invites the response of the reader and therefore risks rejection by the reader.

The purpose of the book is to be part of the celebration of the ten years of Aston. We believe something worthwhile has been achieved in preparing for ordination those candidates who do not fit into the normal pattern. It is far more than a course for thick-oes. It is certainly not 'pre-theological' training for, as will appear, it is profoundly theological and we believe it makes a valuable contribution to theological education not only of ordinands but also for lay people in general. It may even be of interest to other forms of adult education and training from which we have learned much. We want you the reader to enjoy our story of our journey and find that it chimes with your story of your journey, and in some measure adds to it. We want you to share with us in thanking God for it.

If only there were a way of presenting our material which would make the medium part of the message! If Aston is a 'college without walls' should we produce 'leaves without a cover'? But it was too difficult and time-consuming. As so often in running the scheme we have had to make do with the most that is possible for the time being, something that gives us a temporary *platform* from which to construct the next *stage*. Perhaps the second decade will be celebrated with a video tape or an interactive computer program, or whatever has replaced our present technology by then. But nothing can replace the inner reality of the fruits of the Spirit (love, joy, peace, patience, kindness, goodness, fidelity, gentleness and self-control) within personal relationship, shared vocation, exploration of our faith by individual and corporate reflection, genuine penitence and forgiveness, and of what it means, despite our failings, to share Christ's ministry in the world as part of the whole purpose and mission of God, and to be drawn into the life of the Trinity.

Perhaps there will be no further record at all, because Aston will appear, together with Kelham, Knutsford and the rest of its ancestors as part of the history of the next, and by then current, method of education and training within vocation.

Chapter 2 gives a brief history of some of the previous ways of this kind of preparation for Christian ministry and the emergence and growth of ATS. In Chapter 3 we describe what we are trying to do and how we are trying to do it. Because assessment must be in parallel with training, Chapter 4 describes what we believe is a major contribution to assessment procedures within the Church and perhaps in other traditions as well. Our 'college without walls' is held together and enabled to function by its caring and efficient administration described in Chapter 5. There then remain the reflection of Chapter 6 and the visions and dreams of Chapter 7.

Chapter 3 is written by Laurie Green; Chapter 4 by Michael Allen and Chapter 5 in collaboration with Donald Tytler. The rest is by Norman Todd who is responsible for the overall presentation and for the views expressed.

When asked at the planning conference whom they would like to read the book, students gave the following replies.

My Vicar. My Bishop and DDO. Those who are deciding the future pattern of training for ordination. All my friends (from the wife of a student). Adult educators in the Church and also in the secular setting. Members of General Synod. Academic theologians. The theologically oppressed — that is, people whose own experience and ideas are put down by those who think they know best. People who say they could never do that. Those who are being called by God and do not know what the feeling means.

Lastly by way of introduction here are letters from Principals of Theological Colleges, the former now a suffragan bishop.

I have no doubt, whatever, that the students who came to the College from the Aston Training Scheme had benefited enormously from their experience there. One of the ways in which they had benefited might be rather unexpected: the fact that the Bishops' Selectors had recommended that they take the scheme was experienced by them at first as 'failure', and the very fact of having to come face to face with themselves and their reaction to this experience meant in almost every case a deepening in spirituality, self-awareness and general maturity. Most of them came to see that the decision to take the Aston Scheme had in fact been right for them, and felt better equipped to undertake the course at College as a result of it. They also benefited from having remained at work in the secular sphere during their Aston training. Not only did this make for a greater realism and an ability to 'earth' their theology in the light of their previous experience, but it also enabled them to appreciate deeply the opportunity of undertaking full time study at College. Most of our Aston students proved to be academically able, several of them taking the degree course which we offered in conjunction with the local university. Most of them fitted in quickly and easily into the life of the community, and most of them played a useful and often major part in the life of the community (several of them served on the executive committee of the Common Room, and a few became President). In short, I would like to express my personal indebtedness to the Aston Training Scheme for the contribution which its students made to the life of the College, and I was pleased that we had a steady trickle of Aston students each year.

And the second, a newly appointed Principal who gives the impression of his staff.

It is considered that the ex-Aston folk are notably mature in their attitudes as students and particularly open in their approach to assessment. It is also felt that they were noticeably aware of their emotions and relatively honest in their ability to look at themselves, their gifts and their difficulties. The ability to be self-analytical has in some cases led them to being 'too introspective'. One member of staff also felt that as a group of students they were noticeably free and mature in their ability to express friendship and fellowship by touch — I hasten to add that he meant this in an entirely positive way! I hope this is of some help. From my own experience of the Aston Training Scheme and talking with the two products at present I am clear that the assessment system has been of real significance.

2
STARTING

Antecedents

The Church of England has always been identified closely with the ancient universities and has depended on them, and now the modern universities as well, to provide the basic education of its clergy. It was assumed that a university degree was the necessary preliminary to ordination. After an interview with the bishop the man was ordained and then sent to learn how to be a clergyman from a senior curate under the supervision of his rector or vicar. The path to ordination was via university. Later, Theological Colleges as well as providing vocational training for graduates also provided the basic teaching for those who had not been to university. By the last quarter of the nineteenth century it was beginning to be realised that there might be other sources of supply. Herbert Kelly, in his account of the early history of the Society of the Sacred Mission, which he founded, refers to a consciousness in the 1880s that 'we were not doing our work, that we were at most only holding our ground'. By the time he was writing (1908) he could assume that all Church people were very much alive to the 'Dearth of Clergy' in the Mission Field and at home.

'We could not help knowing,' Kelly wrote, 'that there were at the very same time multitudes of men longing to serve, losing faith and hope, because, having no means to pay for an education, they had no opportunity. There must be multitudes still greater, if only we could find the opportunity, the way to inspire, to reach and to use them.' It was to train men for the Mission Field that Kelly founded his Society. They came from elementary schools and would have become clerks had they not been called to the rigorous life of training in the embryo Society. Kelly states: 'As regards the training, the educational results were not only good, but surprisingly good. The men were extraordinarily keen and intensely interested. They were not picked men, and yet they learned to think independently, and to read for themselves intelligently.'

It was not only in his vision of a potential of so many men denied higher education that Kelly was a pioneer. His vision was of Christian

23

ministry freed from 'priestly' interference, and of theology based on 'the great law of induction', and hence of the importance of the right kind of education.

> The way clergy are taught to regard theology not as a view of life, whole in itself and yet complementary to another view, but as a merely technical and professional study, not of essential importance even for their own work, corresponds with, if not directly responsible for, that clerical view of religion as consisting primarily in a particular sphere of observances and emotions in a not very obvious connection with certain accepted opinions and beliefs. The laity have fully accepted the view offered, but with a very different and unclerical estimate of its importance, since, being much occupied with observances in another sphere, they do not find the emotions required come naturally to them . . . It is the first business of the clergy to teach, to show how Christianity bears on life, explains it. The least we can do is to see that they learn their business. (Herbert Kelly SSM, *An Idea in the Working*, Kelham 1953)

This recognition of both the potential of people without formal higher education and of the need to train them in ways which kept them close to their roots in everyday life has been a recurrent theme in the tradition of which Aston Training Scheme is the most recent representative. It was apparent in those who established the Ordination Testing School for ex-servicemen after the First World War. It started in the old prison at Knutsford. In his foreword to its short history by R. V. H. Burne, the first Principal (F. R. Barry, later Bishop of Southwell) wrote:

> It was a great dream come now true. It was born in the faith and vision of Tubby Clayton in his ministry at Toc H, where he began to enlist and enrol servicemen whose war-time experience had led them to turn their thoughts towards Holy Orders. The list grew steadily throughout the war, on all fronts and in all the Services, till it contained many hundreds of names. Here was a rich offer of service. Could the Church accept it and use it? And, primarily, how could the men be trained? What enabled the dream to come true was the steadfast backing of Archbishop Davidson and his 'pledge' of financial help for training, which the Church duly and generously honoured. (That was the first declaration of a policy now universally acknowledged.)

Of the beginning of this 'Ordination Test School' in 1919 Burne wrote:

> The four weary years of war were over and we were free to set out on a joyous adventure to which we believed God was calling us. The war which was to end war had been won, and now we were free to build instead of to destroy. Under the inspiring leadership of the Chief [F. R. Barry] and with the sense of power begotten of fellowship, we believed that we should be able to make

an impact on the Church of England and bring it new life and a more up-to-date outlook. The world was at our feet. Were we to blame for our high spirits? 'Hot air and horse play' some critic called it. But 'Where there is no vision the people perish', and though we may have lived to see the vision fade into the common light of day, it was good to have had it. Let it be said at once that Knutsford gave us something which has become a permanent possession and is with us still. We knew ourselves, in some sense, pioneers. (R.V. H. Burne, *Knutsford*, SPCK 1960)

The principle had been accepted that men could be prepared by the Church before they went forward to the normal training for ordination. There was a Committee on Non-Graduate Training, subsequently becoming a Working Party, and it was from this that plans issued after the Second World War. It was agreed that the aim would be to provide basic literacy and abilities in the techniques of study and that such theology as was taught would be without an examination and aimed at encouraging interest rather than preparing for the General Ordination Examination. Thus the next antecedent of Aston came into being at Brasted.

The prospectus of Brasted Place College describes it as 'a country house of historical interest, standing in its own grounds, near Westerham in Kent'. 'The two year course is followed by a further two years at a Theological College.' 'Although no passes of GCE are required absolutely, yet the possession of a number of GCEs far from barring a man from Brasted is likely to give him a better chance of being accepted. It is equally important to realise that a really good and clearly intelligent man who has no passes in GCE will stand an excellent chance of acceptance for Brasted.' The first year consisted mainly of a course of Christian Humanism under a Lay Tutor, at one time Leslie Paul, and was also a time of further testing of vocation and ability. Students were interviewed by Assessors who decided whether they should continue for the second year during which they would sit for up to three papers of the General Ordination Examination. There were no grants available from Central Church Funds for the maintenance of wives and families. Married men had to find their own accommodation.

Again there was the strong sense of fellowship, the feeling of being pioneers, the attempt to present theology and ministry in a more 'up-to-date' way. There was the shame of having to go to Brasted and the pride of having been there, with some disillusion when Theological College was finally reached. There was the mix of Church traditions and the opportunity for a more creative type of education than the formal lecture. Parallel with Brasted there was the Bernard Gilpin Society in Durham, concentrating on giving ordination candidates the A-Levels they had not been able to take at school, or from which they had not been able to benefit, and doing it within the setting of a Christian community. It also found it was helping them to relate their secular studies to their often new found Christian faith.

A flurry of activity by ACCM committees, working parties, proposals, Governors' meetings ('...received the decision with dismay and astonishment...') and visits resulted in the proposal in 1974 that the two pre-Theological Colleges be merged on one site, which was to be at Brasted and not Durham. The constitution of this new college stated its purpose: to provide a setting in which selected ordinands are enabled to prepare for their subsequent training in a Theological College. It was to be flexible in both content and method, and to seek to encourage growth in the life of prayer and worship and in personal relationships. Its aim was to be a Christian community in both its academic work and its corporate life—and to seek to create in its students personal growth, rather than conformity, and the discovery of truth rather than indoctrination.[1]

Emergence

The establishment of this new college—Ian Ramsey College—was overtaken by doubts about the value for money of residential training, and by a reduction in the number of suitable candidates. Some people thought it best for candidates to work within the normal provision of Colleges of Further Education, some fought strongly for residential training, and a growing number favoured a Church-run non-residential course. Verbal accounts suggest that in the proceedings of both ACCM and of the House of Bishops it was touch and go whether the big change would be made. The story is told how an ACCM meeting was adjourned early for lunch in order that members could be lobbied by enthusiasts for the new scheme. Eventually the ACCM recommendation was accepted by the Bishops, who issued the following statement to the public.

---

[1] Information and quotations are from the relevant files made available by the Archivist of General Synod.

PRE-THEOLOGICAL TRAINING

At its meeting on 8th November the House of Bishops again considered a future pattern for pre-theological training in the Church of England in view of the closure of Ian Ramsey College at Brasted in July 1977.

The House gave approval in principle to proposals for non-residential pre-theological training for men who do not possess the normal educational qualifications but who are recommended for such training by a Bishops' Selection Conference. The details of the scheme are not yet fully worked out, as the Bishops have asked ACCM to consider this matter and to report to the January meeting of the House.

The broad proposal is for a two year course, and it is based on the assumption that the candidate is in full time employment. There will, however, be residential elements in the form of weekends and a longer period in the summer so that all the candidates will experience some of the benefits of community life.

Although the basic syllabus will be moderated by the Advisory Council for the Church's Ministry through a Course Principal, the responsibility for tuition will lie with the man's diocesan officers who will appoint a personal tutor in consultation with the Principal.

The aim will be to preserve some at least of what has been found to be of value in Ian Ramsey College and its predecessors. This has been described as 'the opening of windows of mind and spirit, the stimulating of theological imagination and mental quest'.

By encouraging the development of this form of pre-theological training the House of Bishops wishes to affirm that the Church of England is keenly interested in seeking ordinands among men from all strata of society who, for various reasons, do not possess the normal educational qualifications.

Behind this bland announcement there lay, as always in the Church of England, that flurry of activity. People had been coming together and discovering that their visions overlapped sufficiently for them to get something done about the overlap. The process was in many ways similar to that which produced Kelham, Knutsford, Brasted and Bernard Gilpin, with the difference — which was to become very important — that now ACCM was directly involved in planning, setting up, administering and monitoring the scheme. Mark Green, Bishop of Aston, had been one of the assessors of Brasted students and became chairman of the ACCM Working Party on the Future of Pre-Theological Education, whose report lay behind the Bishops' announcement. He was a parish priest at heart and one of the few clergy who had not been to a Theological College. He was convinced of the potential for effective ministry among men (and later, women) who were outside the main

27

stream of ordinands. They must not be treated as second-best. He was also convinced that theology should be taught in such a way as to avoid the gap which so often developed between it and the daily life of ordinary people. Theology, he insisted, should be done 'on the streets'. This did not mean decrying academic theology, but seeing it through the experience of daily living. He also believed that the assessment procedure he had known at Brasted should be changed completely. Instead of having each man in for twenty minutes rather like an interview for a job, assessment should be basically self-assessment with the candidate increasingly coming to know himself and deciding with the assessors what was best for him.

Working closely with Mark Green on the Working Party was the ACCM Secretary Huw Thomas, who had also been Clerk to the Governors of Brasted. He describes how he suddenly thought that they should forget the idea of a residential college and have two years non-residential on the pattern of the Open University. After discussing it with colleagues he took the idea to the Working Party, and found that it chimed with the ideas of Bishop Mark Green and the other members (Robert Langley and Peter Wheatley). It is his view that the Bishops, feeling rather ashamed of the way Ian Ramsey College had been closed, were ready to clutch at any straw. They did however insist that it should run with one trial batch of candidates and with a part time Principal. The Governing Body of the new Course was to be a sub-committee of ACCM and to be serviced by the resources of General Synod. Now the time had come to find a part time Principal of the right ability and with an understanding of the kind of education that was required.

The post was advertised. However, standing in a bus queue, Huw Thomas was spotted by an old friend, Robin Bennett, driving past on his way to preach in his former parish where Huw now lived in the curate's house. During coffee after the service Huw asked if Robin knew anyone who could apply for a half time post to lead a small experiment in ministry training. 'It seemed to me immediately,' Robin writes, 'that I was myself well qualified and in need of a secure half time salary. I therefore asked to be sent the paperwork, and in due course I was interviewed and appointed.'

Robin Bennett had left his parish to become deputy director of the Urban Ministry Project (UMP) in 1975. This had as its twin bases Ripon Hall, a Theological College in Oxford, and St Peter's parish in Morden, South London. It combined in-service training for clergy with urban experience for theological students, giving them liturgical experiment, some theology and some social analysis, with a chance to meet each other. It included a situation analysis of their job (or of a placement for the students), a visit from the staff and a conference in which to work through the analyses and to lead towards a decision to do something definite in the light of the Course.

'In 1975,' writes Robin, 'as part of the ACCM reorganisation Ripon Hall joined with another Theological College in Oxford, to form the present Ripon College, Cuddesdon. It was a painful time for almost everyone. The college sponsored with UMP a new body called the Oxford Institute for Church and Society, and I was its first Director.' As is often the case the rather grand title cloaked a very insecure organisation. The salary was paid by UMP from funds raised from well-wishers, and there was never more than two or three months' salary in the bank. It was a nerve-racking situation for someone who had been a young but senior incumbent for some years (and a member of General Synod) and had his family to house in Oxford. This was the situation which led Robin to apply for the post of half time Principal of what was to become the Aston Training Scheme. The salary was assured from ACCM, though only for the experimental year.

At the interview for the job there were two applicants. The members of the interviewing panel felt that one candidate had the better teaching qualifications, having been on the staff of a Theological College and also done some adult education in the Church. The other was Robin Bennett, who impressed them with the way he had thought through how he would tackle the work. They were undecided whether to play safe or to take the risk. They would sleep on it and see how it looked next day. Then they took the risk and appointed Robin Bennett, though they all felt it was a risk.

Robin's memory of that interview is that he had done a lot of preparation.

> I found quite a lot of similarities between what the new scheme needed and what I was already doing. These included the following:
> Face to face work with individuals,
> Visits to them at home,
> The learners take responsibility for their own learning,
> The need to give confidence to those who do that learning,
> The use of groups so that people teach one another,
> The integration of personal development and learning how to think, or as I would say today, the use of affective and cognitive modes of learning as supportive of each other.

To recover confidence seemed to me to be the heart of the thing. Many of the new recruits were going to feel that they had failed at school; others that they had failed in relationships. I thought I had detected signs of over-compensation in students from both Bernard Gilpin and Brasted, so I put that high on the list. But there was also the question of how to give the C of E confidence in this source of new recruits. I felt it worthwhile to try and get the Open University to give block entrance to the new scheme. And then, thirdly, there was the problem of money.

At no time was he on a contract of more than two years; the first budget was minuscule, and finance for each new year had to be fought through.

The new Course had emerged from the overlap of visions: a concern for clergy and their training; a theology on the street; the way people learn; a non-residential education combining the insights of adult education, group work and theology. Bridget Edger, the one person who has been on the staff of the Course for its whole ten years, was working half time, having previously been on the staff of Ripon Hall. The Governing Body, with Bishop Mark Green as Chairman, Huw Thomas as Secretary, and with Ann Cameron, another former Assessor at Brasted and a member of General Synod, a strong supporter of the new project, discussed what it should be called.

That Mark Green wanted to call it 'Brasted without walls' indicates both the importance of the work that had gone before and something of the outgoing explorative nature of the spirit in which it was conceived. Others suggested 'Green College' and finally settled for 'The Aston Training Scheme', because Mark Green was Bishop of Aston.

Growth

'I began,' Robin remembers, 'by getting to know people.' This meant both the administrators and the students, of whom there were seven. Before he visited the students he had to ring the administrator at ACCM to ask if he could claim the rail fare on expenses – it was as experimental as that.

'I met students in their homes and developed a method of visiting that owed quite a lot to UMP. I tried to have three hours with the student and his wife. It was soon obvious that single students were not helped by having parents present. I tried from the beginning to include wives in the conversation and soon got adept at being practical – it will take so many evenings a week, so many weekends, etc. It took all my powers of patience and explanation; there was sometimes hostility, more often puzzlement and sheer panic at the thought of having to do all that study when often the person hadn't read a book. I found myself buttering them up to increase their confidence at least to have a go. I met suspicious vicars who wanted to help, and sometimes to protect, their student. I met students who wanted to know why they had to study when St Peter had started straightaway on the shore of Galilee.

'I quickly discovered that the students divided into three groups. There were those who were reasonably mature and were prepared to do anything to qualify, and who knew they needed help. Others were not very mature nor with very much academic experience, and rather resented having to do the scheme. The third group were immature but academically quite well qualified and thought they ought to go straight to college. Across these three bands were the churchmanship convictions, most of them coming from the Anglo-Catholic or evangelical wings of the Church. People from the broad stream were very few.

'I went to see the Open University in Oxford and in Milton Keynes. The academic staff were marvellous. Eventually we got block entry to the A 101 course, the Arts Foundation, but it lasted only one year because the OU abandoned all block entries. Then I brought in OU tutors and materials and even set up our own OU Summer School using the three or four local tutors we had come across. They were so helpful. They liked the scheme and would write to me and ask me to meet them and discuss what we were trying to do. I found that they approached the problems of teaching in quite a new way. The emphasis was on how people can be helped to learn. In a similar way the National Extension College in Cambridge helped me a lot and we employed their *Return to Study* course from the beginning. The joy of the OU and NEC courses was the way they used literature to help students learn about life — life then, or life now, personal perceptions, what it feels like to be the character of fiction, or the writer.

'The first weekend was in autumn 1977. The highlight was a visit, the first of many, to a theatre, this time to see *Pygmalion* at the Birmingham Rep. The next day we had a discussion about it, and I think it was that which gave the Governors confidence that we would be OK, as they could see that students were already getting down to work. We went to church; we had planning meetings for study; we felt we were doing something new and found it both exciting and nerve-racking as there were so many unanswered questions. I also included a meeting of the student common room, and from the first tried to take it seriously. They in fact organised their own extra weekend at a Christian holiday home. I was a bit nervous about this, thinking that they might form defensive cliques, but now I think I was wrong; they taught one another, and out of the weekend came the famous Aston Fellowship

'Very quickly I began to form a staff group, and this for three reasons. One was my need to do team teaching. Despite my strongly held convictions, many of which arise out of intuition and are thought through afterwards, I have a strong streak of self-doubt and always do better with a supportive company around me. The second was a straightforward understanding that we needed a range of skills wider than one man could provide. I was, and am, a sort of entrepreneurial fixer, or as Peter Baelz once called me, a sort of honest broker. Better not try to do everything myself. The third reason for a staff was to make the students feel safe — that is to have a person of their own churchmanship present whenever we met for a weekend. The chapel came to be a real focus — a place to pray in and to put one's burden on the Lord, but also an ecclesiastical battleground where such matters as bowing, dress, leadership style in worship, absence of familiar landmarks, etc., etc., were all a great worry and burden on the student who happened to feel difficult that weekend. The first weekend of any year was a particular moment of stress, and I can remember one student nearly going home from a particularly high-profile Roman Catholic retreat house simply because it offended him to see the Anglo-Catholic students loving it. Fraught it was! but he became one of our best students, partly because we held him that weekend.

'So the staff team, for the reasons mentioned, came to consist of several specialists: a practical parish-based theologian, a teacher of the Bible, someone with insight into the Gospel's relevance to the city, and someone who could facilitate personal growth. Then there were vicars with badges, a very straight evangelical, one from the inner city, and a Catholic from Liverpool. This team was a marvellous group and we all knew it — we had some fabulous staff meetings, sometimes for twenty-four hours, sometimes just for the day. They came to the weekends as best they could; they sometimes brought their wives with them, and they came with their skill or their conviction. They gelled, and as well as planning we shared our ideas about learning and the direction of theology in a way which we all found inspiring. Later on this changed and was less good. Probably it was simply that we stopped pioneering and became more a management group. Bishop Mark came as spiritual adviser and we tried to find a deaconess to join us.

'Meanwhile Aston was moving and growing. Being a college without walls, rather like the Hebrew tabernacle in the wilderness, was not a settled existence, but the lack of any restriction of buildings meant that we could cope with the very fast increase in those recommended to join the scheme. This was a great encouragement to the instigators, although it did occasionally produce its moments of panic. From an intake of eighteen students in October 1977, the scheme suddenly grew to fifty in October 1978 with a second intake of thirty-two. The first weekend that year was for the whole scheme and the unexpected increase in numbers was highlighted by the fact that in order to be able to ask as many wives to come with their husbands as wished, we had to ask them if they minded sharing single rooms for the weekend.'

Over the next few years the yearly intake averaged out as thirty, and this meant that by 1979 and 1980 there were approximately sixty students on the scheme at any one time. In 1980 the administrative centre moved from a former vicarage in the middle of Oxford to Westminster College on the outskirts of that city, which gave some additional office space. But it also became obvious that Robin Bennett needed some additional regular staff help and Bill Ind, who had already been helping on the staff team at some weekends, was appointed as part time Vice-Principal. The basis of his appointment was that the scheme paid his diocese a sum which enabled Bill to come to all the residential weekends and Summer Schools as well as to do some visiting of students in the south. Bill's regular presence at the residential occasions was a great strength and support both to Robin and also to the students, as can be seen from some of the comments from students.

A former student remembers this time:

Bill Ind was an extremely lively man with a zest for anything he introduced. He was a Catholic whose interest in theology was infectious and he joined in heartily with everything, be it Benediction, an impromptu cricket match or a contribution to the homespun entertainment that marked the end of Summer School.

Neville Black is remembered by many students as the man they found most provocative and disturbing. Prophetic, very blunt, never mincing his words. Neville stood four-square in his Everton parish, in the round hole of the Church of England. He challenged the values and assumptions of students, upsetting quite a few who had never encountered the realities of inner city life. He was brave, and had plenty of guts to challenge us then as *Faith in the City* should be disturbing the Church and nation today.

Tony Barnard seemed, in contrast, an academic who gave his time unsparingly to introduce students to the shock of biblical criticism. I can still remember the horror of some students as they realised that his theology was poles apart from their own. More than mental arithmetic was needed to resolve the question of how many animals of each kind went into Noah's Ark.

All three men somehow made time, from their already over-busy lives, to train students on the scheme. They gave of their meagre leisure time and the scheme and the Church has much to thank them for.

The move to Westminster College was in fact only to be for a year, for during the latter part of 1980 and early 1981 wide discussions took place about the need for another full time member of staff (which would mean the need for increased office space) and also the possibility of the Aston Centre being in a more central and appropriate place than Oxford. Various options were explored, including, due to financial pressure, the appointment of the new member of staff being combined with another part time church post, but the Governing Body finally came to the conclusion that the best suggestion had been made by the Bishop of Birmingham, that the Principal should be appointed as priest-in-charge of St Peter's, Springhill (with a full time curate), and that the Aston Centre and the Principal's home should be in St Peter's Vicarage. At the same time it was agreed to appoint a full time Director of Studies.

So, in September 1981, Robin Bennett and Bridget Edger gave up their homes in Oxford and moved with the scheme to Birmingham — Robin to live in St Peter's Vicarage and Bridget buying her own home on the outskirts of Birmingham and working in the Vicarage. At the same time, following his appointment in July, Alec Knight took up his appointment as Director of Studies. In fact his first job with the scheme was putting up the bookshelves in Robin's study in the Vicarage.

Unfortunately, the vision of basing Aston in an inner city Birmingham parish with the Principal working in the parish as well as with the scheme, and with the very busy Aston office in the same building as Robin and his family's home, could not withstand the pressures of reality, and the strain was too great. As Robin says: 'I found myself unable to cope. I went sick, and recovered slowly. While I was away on retreat, I wrote to Bishop Mark (now my Bishop as well as Chairman of the Aston Governors) and resigned the benefice — a cause of great upset, I fear.' Added to the pressures of the two jobs was the fact that Bridget had to go into hospital in November and was away from the office for three months. Also the understandably difficult, essential but time-consuming process of expanding a full time staff team of two into three had to be coped with. While Robin was away sick, Alec, having only joined the scheme five months before, and Bridget found themselves supporting each other in holding the scheme together. But it was only for a short time, as Robin recovered and then the whole question of where in Birmingham Aston was now to be based could be raised. Robin was able to negotiate a move to Westhill College of Education in Selly Oak. He was ready to start again. But he did not start again at Aston. He applied for, and was appointed to, a job in the Board of Education of General Synod concerned with Adult Education.

John Oddy, then about to become the ACCM secretary with special responsibility for the Aston Scheme, writes:

> In spring 1981, just before I entered Aston's world, the scheme was thrown prematurely into its adolescence by the fateful decision to move its HQ to Springhill, Birmingham. The plan, born in part of nostalgia and the search for roots, had an artificial glamour whilst at the same time heavily over-stretching resources and especially so the human ones. Nonetheless it was probably the pain of that year in Springhill which opened the door for the move into the second generation and adult life of the scheme.

Alec Knight and Bridget Edger moved the Aston Centre over to Westhill College in September, where it was to have a secure base for three years. However, as a result of no appointment being made after the first advertisement for a new Principal, for the next eight months Alec, with a total student body of sixty-five, was again the only full time academic member of staff in the role of acting-Principal. It was only the support and generous offers of time from the part time staff team that kept the scheme going. Bridget remembers 'feeling as though I was holding Alec up, while he held Aston up. But I also remember a lot of laughter and feelings of shared achievement through that winter. But then, those are the things that I remember feeling through all my time with Aston. That is what makes working with the scheme so exciting and fulfilling.'

The task of appointing a new Principal was urgent and, in the interviewing process for candidates, Aston students were to be involved for the first time. The second advertisement of the post led to a formal interviewing panel together with a less formal group comprising part time staff, Aston students and Bridget meeting the candidates. The appointment of Laurie Green as Principal brought a number of new resources to the scheme. He had extensive experience in group work and long exposure to inner city ministry at Spaghetti Junction, Birmingham, where his concern to enable the laity to fulfil their ministry had produced an important piece of work, soon to be published. His own philosophy of education – reciprocity between teacher and taught – fitted with the style of Alec Knight, while his emphasis on affirmation of the student gave a new dimension to the scheme.

With a new Principal in post, some of the part time staff felt it was the right time to leave, having been Robin's personal support. At this point Mark Green also resigned the chairmanship, feeling that the scheme was once again secure and ready for a new lease of life under the new Principal. There was lots of work to do, and with a new group of part time staff also being created the task of team-building was very important. The new group was an attempt firstly to increase the number of teaching staff for weekends but secondly also to provide a variety of models and skills. Laurie brought in people he already knew and people he didn't know in order to build a team of expertise rather than a support team. So the people who joined and gave their time and energy brought with them experience of urban and rural ministry; of middle class suburban ministry; theological expertise; awareness of confronting in their own persons the issues of class, racism and sexism; experience from the Lutheran Church and from the Orthodox Churches; learning skills and adult education practice; views from all parts of the Church in terms of worship styles; and much more. Forming a team from such diverse and sometimes divergent interests was not simple, and the growth that there was came as much out of struggle as from acceptance. Previously the staff had been seen both by students and by themselves as being very separate from the student body, but now the barriers were being broken down, allowing more openness and vulnerability on both sides.

After a few months Alec moved on to take up the new challenge of parochial ministry and the full time Aston staff was back to two. Although the Governing Body wanted to make a swift appointment of a new Director of Studies to ease the burden, Laurie and Bridget carried on together by themselves for a whole year. This was done in order to give Laurie a chance to find out what the Principal's job was and could become, and it gave Bridget time to feel affirmed in her new role as Administrator. Throughout that year the ACCM Inspectors were around, and this gave a sharpness to the issues that might not have been noticed so much without them. Laurie used this time, as he puts it, 'to feel the whole weight of Aston' so as to know where the balancing point was. It was to help in deciding the internal structure and also the pattern of student weekends and work.

When the time came to appoint a second member of the educational staff Laurie knew that his prime need was for a Vice-Principal who was a good and Christian person and who could cope with the hierarchical structure and the collegiate style of working. Michael Allen brought with him a more Protestant style of Anglicanism to counter-balance Laurie's more Catholic stance, and many pastoral skills. His particular skill with individuals in both listening and caring and then getting down to the issues was very strong — he was a probing counsellor but in a very affirmative way — which gave the scheme new depths. As soon as he arrived he himself undertook an OU course on adult education and then took on the project work, a piece of work that had originated with Laurie, and brought it to fruition.

The opening up of the full time staff team from two to three could have posed more difficulties, but didn't. Bridget in particular records how much easier it was than she feared it might be. Both Laurie and Michael brought with them the experience born of many years in tough parishes where a collegial style had operated, and now they, together with Bridget, worked on building up the scheme which had so nearly foundered.

For two years these three developed the affirmative yet tough style of working with students that the scheme has become known for. The philosophy is explained further in the next two chapters, but for now it can be described as student-centred, loving, even tender, but not soft. Students are built up and challenged as people whom God has called to ministry.

In search of more space the scheme moved headquarters in spring 1985 across the road to Central House of the Selly Oak Colleges. From the summer of 1985 it became apparent that rising numbers meant another increase in staff. A part time post of Tutor was advertised, but before it was filled the staff and Governors realised it must be full time, and that finance was available. Someone was needed who could complement the other full time academic staff both in terms of skill and experience — someone with academic strengths but with a commitment to the adult education philosophy already being used; with experience in study skills and distance learning evaluation. Jeni Parsons was appointed in May and took up her post in September 1986. She brought experience of working in the Church as a lay person and in particular as a lay woman, and came with a great deal of expertise in the area of experiential Christian adult education. The new post was for a Tutor, but it soon became apparent that this title was being misunderstood by outsiders and by some students as indicating a purely academic role, whereas Jeni now had responsibility for the first year students in pastoral, academic and spiritual matters. Her title is still undecided since suitable alternatives are not easy to find.

Again there is a need for renewed team building. The full time staff has grown to four and such teams need time to learn how to work together. Only by paying careful attention to this area can any good work be done in the scheme. If we expect openness and honesty from the students then we also expect it from each other, and that isn't cheap, but comes at the price of vulnerability and risk but also with the generating of excitement and opportunity.

This is nearly the end of ten years' history and it is right that it should be told in terms of the people involved, since Aston isn't *anywhere* but is comprised of the hopes and aspirations of many people who connect to form a network called the Aston Training Scheme. How that is held together can be found in Chapter 5. We finish this chapter with the views of two people outside the scheme, both Open University tutors.

I owe my initial involvement with Aston to my university friendship with Robin Bennett, who heard that I worked for the OU and got me involved. I did not actually need any persuading for I was vocationally committed to the aims of the OU and acutely aware that the Church of England needed something like Aston. I was paying an acknowledged debt to my late father, who, after leaving elementary school at fourteen due to parental poverty, and beginning work as a farm labourer, eventually was helped to attend Theological College in Oxford as a day boy.

As a full-timer in higher and adult education until recently, I was always impressed by the calibre of our Aston students and their ability to arrange crowded lives to make this study and the Aston commitments possible. I admire so much so many of these students who used to give up their annual summer holiday for this experience. Every Summer School saw me returning thinking the ordained ministry of the C of E was in good hands. Now that I am once more in the full time parish life, I believe it still and put the Aston Summer School at the top of the list of extra-parochial responsibilities.

¶ My introduction to the Aston Scheme was a gentle one. As an Open University tutor in Social Sciences I was approached to see if some Aston students could sit in on my classes and have their work assessed by me. The prospect was exciting, but more than a little daunting: I had no idea what to expect. What would they be like, these trainees for the priesthood? I'd never known anyone in the Church, and had no idea what their expectations of me would be. Were they going to stick out like sore thumbs, these little children of God? I need have had no fear; they were just like any other OU student following a new road whilst juggling with the other commitments of life. I soon got more involved.

The question of an Aston Social Science Summer School came up. For those Aston students not in the OU one would have to be devised. We decided on a programme of work as close to the OU model as possible. This was difficult but in the end really worthwhile. I had felt for some time that Social Science had not been given enough weight in the programme. This was because they did it in the second year without time to finish before they went on to Theological College. I feel though that this also reflected the relatively new awareness that an understanding of the nature and dynamic of the society in which students will be entering Ministry is an essential component of theological training. My campaigning on behalf of the Social Sciences matched a growing concern among Aston staff and students that the second year programme was not as appropriate as it might be. I was invited to contribute to a specifically designed second year programme which would include an eight week introduction to the Social Sciences. This was to be a written distance learning text with a weekend residential workshop. By burning a phenomenal amount of midnight oil, the course was completed for a trial run in 1985 and fully operational in 1986. The deadlines were so tight that I regularly used my own version of express delivery: I would get to work at 8 am, photocopy the typescript of the night before and then take it round to a friend who worked in the House of Commons (having stamped the envelope). She would then post it in the House's post, which ensured a next morning delivery in Birmingham. This proved foolproof, even in the Christmas rush. My friends thought I was quite mad during this period, as I would work on the course during every spare moment. This was, curiously, quite productive of ideas.

I would say, from the first full series of workshops and assessments this year, that the course has been successful. We have certainly raised some central issues and had some passionate classroom discussions. We have also seen and experienced Birmingham's inner ring, what used to be called the twilight zone. We have worshipped there, eaten in the local cafes and drunk in the local pubs. We tried, in an uncomfortably brief way, to touch the reality of the inner city. *Faith in the City* argues that Christians should do much more. I hope our sessions opened a few eyes, challenged a few preconceptions, for that is what an educational process should aim to do.

For me personally, Aston has been rewarding and enriching. I too have opened my eyes and had my preconceptions challenged. I wish Aston well for the next ten years.

3
TRYING TO DO IT

It was recognised that if students were to develop study skills and confidence in academic work, then ways would have to be found to introduce appropriate courses into the syllabus which could be followed mainly in their own homes and localities. The Aston Scheme could not provide the support and back-up which has turned the old-fashioned 'correspondence courses' into the more substantial and effective 'distance learning' which the best adult education institutions now provide. So Aston had to look outward to see if such a nationwide network existed already elsewhere. It was possible for students to study GCE courses at local evening classes but whereas O- and A-Level courses were primarily designed for school pupils, the Open University courses were specifically geared to the domestic and educational needs of adults. These courses, then, could provide the initial backbone of the syllabus and between these could be slotted a course of introduction to the Bible, borrowed from another theological course, and a short introduction to study skills bought in from the National Extension College. This very simple but effective means of study sufficed for some years while the other elements of the syllabus were being devised and developed.

From the experience of the Assessors who had worked at Brasted and Ian Ramsey College, it had been learned that the usual methods of Anglican assessment were very deficient. A few short interviews and reports at the end of the course simply provided insufficient evidence upon which to decide the fate of each candidate. The Assessors who were appointed to Aston were under the leadership of Mark Green, the Bishop of Aston, and had personal experience of the scanty methods of assessment used elsewhere. They therefore set about developing a method of continuous assessment which, after mid-term written reports, climaxed at the end of the course in a thorough self-assessment and report-writing programme. It was an innovation which was to prove devastatingly productive as an educational tool, as a method of ministerial formation and as a means of assessment for the Church.

If students were expected to undertake such rigorous studies at home, if they were to experience the tough self-assessment programme and, in addition, gain from all the residential gatherings which the new course entailed, there had to be opportunity for the student to reflect upon all this experience personally and at some significant depth. For this purpose, each student was to be found a local Pastoral Tutor with whom they would be expected to meet on a monthly basis for an in depth two-hour conversation. There too all other aspects of the student's life and experience would be reflected upon and, it was hoped, a clearer perception reached as to what God was wanting of each student.

The Bishops were happy that a student on Aston would need to attend residentially for four weekends each year, in addition to an Open University Summer School and a special Summer Week provided by the scheme itself. On this basis, the Principal gathered around himself a small team of part time volunteers who would assist in the production of educational residential events to guide students through some major themes of Christian life and ministry. Such themes as 'Who am I?', 'Spirituality', 'Work' and 'Doctrine' were selected and experiential educative events designed around each theme by the group. This amalgam of distance learning, study work, Pastoral Tutors, assessment and residential events formed the basic skeleton of the new scheme. The first students arrived hot-foot from their Selection Conference in September 1977 and undertook the syllabus of the very new Aston Training Scheme.

It was this overall design which served students very well during the early years and which was constantly being redeveloped as the scheme gained experience. By 1982, however, it had become clear that considerable modification was necessary. There were clearly many reasons, for example, to rethink the second year of the syllabus. As it stood, it consisted simply of a short biblical course followed by an eight-month Open University course. This latter course did not end until students had already finished with Aston and were well into the first term at their Theological Colleges. This was very unsatisfactory and many students found it impossible to cope with the overlap.

In addition to this, the course seemed to have lost some of its original focus upon Christian faith and ministerial formation, and it was felt by many that Aston was rather vulnerable and shaky. Many hard lessons had been learnt at the cost of much pain and anguish and it was crucial that somehow Aston should capitalise on this experience, recapture its vision, and develop the sort of stability in which students could grow and risk themselves.

The second Principal, Laurie Green, arrived at precisely the right time for a radical reappraisal of the syllabus. Alec Knight, who had been holding the fort during the interregnum, had already made significant progress in sharpening up some elements of the assessment process and had also introduced the basic idea of an induction programme for intending students. Laurie Green arrived with considerable experience of the North American seminary scene and, having just served for ten years as vicar at Spaghetti Junction, Birmingham, was intent on gearing the syllabus more towards the specific needs of Christian ministerial formation. As he was taught the Aston ropes by Alec Knight and Bridget Edger, he had opportunity to assess the programme in the light of recent educational praxis and, perhaps even more significantly, to address the question of the syllabus design theologically.

First it was necessary to reassess the stated aims of the syllabus. It was soon agreed with the Governing Body that the aims should be redrafted to allow more focus upon the contextual nature of the endeavour. A diagrammatic presentation of the newly stated aims was soon developed and agreed with the staff and students. It was a dynamic whirl of four elements, the personal, contextual, academic and vocational (Diagram 1).

The aims were stated more formally thus:

> The scheme aims to help its students gain further experiences in preparation for their formal training at Theological College. It offers help in many areas of the student's life but particularly in the following:
>
> i. Personal growth and self-understanding.
> ii. Academic self-confidence and skill.
> iii. Understanding of one's relationship to the Church and modern society.
> iv. Vocational and spiritual development.
>
> The scheme must be carefully designed to address all these areas and understands them to be intimately and dynamically related. (*Aston Handbook*, p.5)

While these Aston syllabus aims were being clarified, it was possible to develop some theological basis upon which the redevelopment of the syllabus could be constructed. From his work with the development of the Urban Theology Unit syllabus in Sheffield, Laurie Green was convinced that it was possible to run biblical models alongside educational models with exciting consequences. It was found that, by comparing some gospel processes with modern educational and societal parallels, some basic building blocks for a new syllabus could emerge.

Diagram 1

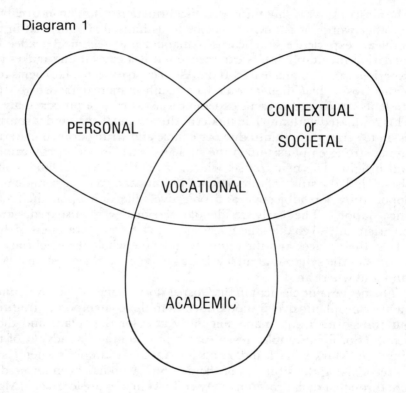

PERSONAL

CONTEXTUAL
or
SOCIETAL

VOCATIONAL

ACADEMIC

Because there was also a real concern to connect the students back into their own localities and groups, notions of locally-based projects and study themes, local support groups and the students' own personal and social journeys became central features of a complete reworking of the course design.

Gospel Process and Course Design

The Gospel story is shot through with affirmation of human incarnation. In other words, it is down to earth. Jesus himself is immersed in the Galilean experience and learns a manual and technical trade. Incarnation inevitably limits experience but it locates it and makes our experience more manageable. If the Aston course was to take cognisance of this Gospel bias then it would have to affirm more demonstrably the students' prior and present experiences as worthy of proper analysis. This resonated with much in modern educational theory and it spurred us on to scrap the old introductory course and write our own material, laying strong emphasis upon the students' early experiences, training and insight. The new course, which was entitled 'New Dimensions', also included a study of the students' locality and gave each student an opportunity for subjective and objective reflection upon their own 'incarnation'. The early residential sessions were also redesigned experientially to enable students to come to a clearer awareness of their selves, their places and their gifts. So now the whole thrust of the first months of the syllabus at all levels was to be upon the questions 'Who am I and where am I?'

The next major element in the Gospel story seemed to be pronouncement or prophetic declaration drawn from the contemporary tradition but transformed and made singularly new for that place and those people. So, for example, Jesus comes proclaiming the advent of the kingdom (Mark 1.14-15 and parallels). Another example is when Jesus, on recognising the situation of the paralytic who has been lowered to him through a roof, proclaims, 'My child, your sins are forgiven' (Mark 2.5 and parallels). This resonates in educational praxis with many of the findings of those who work on making the meaning of a situation of oppression conscious to those who should be liberated from it. In this case, educationalists like Paulo Freire have sought out the 'generative terms or pronouncements' drawn from the people's experience which would inspire them to new consciousness. On Aston, then, the Gospel indicated that we should endeavour to let the students search their traditions and hear and make those statements which would strike in them chords of vocational purpose. It would be necessary to rework the biblical courses appropriately and also encourage students to immerse themselves in those 'traditions' of the arts and social sciences where human beings have sought to discover and express their human predicament. Alongside this would run residential periods where Christian spirituality would be explored and where the penetrating themes of 'Power and Powerlessness' and 'Joy and Sorrow' could be experientially investigated.

The student would at this stage be asked to undertake the redesigned self-assessment process and from that crucible would emerge words and phrases which encapsulated or crystallised the issues which were the major focus of concern for the student in his or her incarnational predicament.

On looking back to the Gospels, the next step in the process seemed to be a concerted working through of the issues thus raised within a group which had been drawn together around the prophetic word. So Jesus' call to repent in view of the advent of the kingdom is worked out within the disciple group. The implications of Jesus' words of forgiveness to the paralytic are worked through with those gathered around Jesus in the house where that healing was occurring. So on Aston there had now to be developed opportunity for students to work concertedly on the words, themes and issues that had come to them from their study of their own incarnation and their new appreciation of the traditions in which they stood. To this end Laurie borrowed an idea to which he had been introduced during his doctoral work in the United States. Each student would be made responsible for the development and maintenance of a local project group, and would study with the group the implications of a theme which had been carefully drawn out from their own personal discovery of gifts and need during the whole Aston experience. Group work, individual work and personally tutored work would be designed to help elucidate actively and reflectively the particular issue that was pertinent to the student as God touched them during the training process.

Time and again in the Gospels this group exploration would issue in a decisive action or moment. Thus, the implications of the kingdom's advent were to be expressed in Cross and Resurrection; the reality of Jesus' words of forgiveness issued in his empowering of the paralytic — 'take up your bed and walk'. Good educational design also demanded that what had been learnt had to be expressed and the students' new

45

place appreciated and felt. In Aston, then, there had to be a place for the new personal assessment and vocational determination to be expressed and fed back to the group and to the wider world. The completion, presentation and celebration of the Project, in which would be included a clear statement of the students' learning and new thrust, would be the springboard at the end of Aston into the next new discovery of God's world and the students' specific incarnation within it.

So the overall redesign of Aston gave it more flow and shape together with renewed Gospel integrity and educational respectability. It used the basic experience which Aston had so far gained, but demanded a thorough reworking of its present components and the introduction of exciting new features. The new design was still based upon Aston's early vision but promised to empower students by introducing the notion of a Gospel release of the potential that lay within them. The alternative was to work from the false premise that there was something 'wrong' with students on the Aston Scheme that was not 'wrong' with ordinands elsewhere.

The new design stemmed from Laurie's ideas but had been successively worked through with the students themselves, with the Aston Governing Body, and then with the ACCM educational advisory bodies. In those early days Laurie used and reworked a flow diagram (Diagram 2) to demonstrate the shape of his background thinking. After careful checking at all levels it was then possible to draw up another chart to indicate how this would be worked out in practice, given all that Aston had so far experienced and learned about training for ministry. A great deal more flexibility was demanded in the Aston structure in order that each student could truly become the centre of the syllabus and agenda, and this required the bringing together of a new staff team committed to struggling with the limitations and realities in order to bring the reworked Aston from its chrysalis.

The New Two-Year Programme

This programme has now been operating with great success for two years, during which it has been under constant review and development. The original reworked design has required very little revision but the teaching team and students have proved amazingly resourceful in finding ways to implement the vision.

It is now necessary to describe in rather more detail the several elements in the overall programme and the reader may find reference to the syllabus flow-diagram (Diagram 3) helpful.

Diagram 2

GOSPEL PROCESS	HUMAN INCARNATION	PROPHETIC DECLARATION	EXPLORATION OF IMPLICATIONS	DECISIVE MOMENT OR MOVEMENT	NEW PLACE
N.T.	SEEING EYE Limitation to contemporary and antecedent history Hellenism/Judaism etc. COMING DOWN TO EARTH	HEARING EAR Immersing in and analysing of the Tradition from experience	debates groups parables trying out 'provisional theologies'	appropriate action setting up change moments	Post Resurrection Church
Examples I	30 years carpenter	'Kingdom of God come'	Disciple group Parables Conflict Parabolic actions	Jerusalem The Cross	Post Resurrection Church
Examples II	Paralysis	'Your sins are forgiven'	'Who but God?'	'Get up and walk!'	
CONTEMPORARY PARALLEL	Situation Analysis Affirmation of experiences as worthy of analysis	'Generative terms' Freire Word event New Paradigms Searching the traditions	Unpacking the relationship between situation and tradition both actively and reflectively	War of position (Gramsci) Appreciation of new perspective Making stories happen Initiating apposite change	War of movement
ASTON	Weekend themes:- 1. 'Who am I?' 2. 'Me in my situation' 3. 'The theology I am working and living by so far' PLUS STUDY SKILL LEARNING AFFIRMATION	Course Work 1. Humanities OU. What people have done to express their human predicament. Weekend Themes Suffering Power Course work/weekends Biblical studies Social Studies Project Theme Week	1. Project Study 2. Local Parish Group work 3. Personal Assessment 4. Weekend theme 'Doctrine'	1. Personal Assessment 2. Project determination 3. Vocational statement 4. Assessment of Aston by student body 5. Diploma	Post Aston 1. Theological college 2. Continuing time before theological college 3. Lay ministry

Diagram 3 **The New Two-Year Syllabus**

APRIL-SEPT.

ACCM recommend student to Aston
INDUCTION DAY at Aston Centre
ASTON PREPARATORY COURSES
available
STAFF VISIT to student's home

> Aston
> Preliminary
> Courses
> available

YEAR I

SEPTEMBER — REGIONAL DAY: review of course

OCTOBER — WEEKEND: STUDY SKILLS & 'WHO AM I?'
Student meets Assessors

NOVEMBER — WEEKEND: MINISTRY & CONTEXT
(whole student body meets together)

JANUARY — WEEKEND: SPIRITUALITY

> THE ASTON
> INTRODUCTORY
> COURSE –
> 'NEW DIMENSIONS'
> incl: Childhood
> Our Roles in Society
> Anglicanism
> The Arts
> Our Communities
> Religious Language

FEBRUARY — Open University Course begins

APRIL — WEEKEND: POWER & POWERLESSNESS

JUNE — Student writes 1st Self-Assessment Letter

JULY — 1. OU SUMMER SCHOOL WEEK
2. ASTON SUMMER SCHOOL WEEK
incl. Mid-term Assessment by Assessors

> OPEN
> UNIVERSITY
> COURSE
>
> usually a
> Foundation Course
> in the Arts or
> Social Sciences

YEAR II

SEPTEMBER — REGIONAL DAY: review of course

OCTOBER — WEEKEND: JOY & SORROW

late OCT. — Sits OU Examination
PAROCHIAL WORK EXPERIENCE

NOVEMBER — WEEKEND: BIBLICAL STUDIES
(whole student body meets together)

FEBRUARY — PROJECT WEEK: PLANNING
Introduction to 'SOCIAL SCIENCES' or
            'THE HUMANITIES TODAY'
LOCAL SUPPORT GROUP WORK

MARCH — WEEKEND: WHAT IS THEOLOGY?
Student writes Final Self-Assessment Letter

MAY — WEEKEND:
THE NATURE OF THE CHURCH
Student meets Assessors for Final Assessment

JUNE — Projects submitted

JULY — ASTON SUMMER SCHOOL WEEK
incl: Project Presentations: Preparing for College:
Aston Certificate

> BIBLE
> INTRODUCTION
> COURSE
>
> SOCIAL SCIENCE
> or HUMANITIES
> COURSE
>
> PROJECT
>
> OR 2nd
> OU COURSE

48

I INDUCTION

Since the scheme does not select its own students but rather receives them from ACCM, the induction process for each student is crucial. There has always been an element of bad feeling about Aston among some incoming students and it was to combat this that Alec Knight began to set up an induction process. Since then, this has been given an increased prominence so that it now receives a great amount of time and energy from the full time staff, especially the Principal. That a student should begin well is understood to have a high priority and to this end the process is elaborate and developmental.

Just as soon as a student is recommended to do Aston, she or he will receive a letter of welcome together with information about the scheme and a registration form. This basic paperwork is only the beginning of the increasing level of contact through which the student passes so that by the end all are, practically and emotionally, engaged in Aston. The student is immediately invited to attend an Induction Day at the Aston office in Birmingham along with about six to ten other students and their partners. This is of use in several ways. It introduces them to each other, to the full time staff and to the building from which Aston operates; it lets them get a feeling of having 'begun' and yet it should not be too overwhelming because the meeting is quite small-scale. At the day they hear the scheme explained and also have time to comment on their own feelings about being on Aston. The day is therefore an introduction to the group work which is such an essential feature of the scheme.

Each student then receives a visit at home from the Principal, lasting up to three hours, at which the agenda for that student's development through Aston is set. Great importance is placed on seeing the students in their own environment and with their family, since that is a very important part of their context and needs to be understood and affirmed by the scheme. The issues arising from the ACCM recommendation are outlined and these also form part of the agenda-setting. The criteria for the choice of a local and personal Pastoral Tutor for the student are also talked through to enable as good a match as possible, taking into account the student's needs and wishes. Wherever possible the student's parish priest is also visited by the Principal on this occasion, and his hopes and fears for the ordinand are gleaned as are his recommendations about the type of Pastoral Tutor needed. Again it is a time to affirm the local context and to explain the Aston vision and process.

After these two visits the Principal writes a long and detailed report which is sent to the Local Director of Ordinands or Lay Ministry Adviser, and through this collaboration the Pastoral Tutor is chosen and appointed by the Principal. Again the diocesan context is affirmed — a part of the original vision but one which has needed working on very much, for many DDOs and DLMAs feel that Aston is breaking new territory. It is very important for the fulfilment of our vision that everyone involved should 'own' what is happening: the student, the parish and the diocese need to feel that they are a part of the Aston process. There has been a careful building up of relationships with DDOs and DLMAs, who know their students well and are also the link back to the candidate's sponsoring bishop. The pastoral side of the relationship with the student which is initiated with the induction process will include continued reference back to the diocese, for it is part of the original vision that the local is taken seriously. Such contact with the diocese is becoming more frequent and works to everyone's advantage. In the past, some DDOs and DLMAs didn't know what Aston was and were sometimes very discouraging to the students. Now, quite a large number are actively committed to Aston, realising what it is trying to do and approving the methods by which it works. The local network of family, parish and diocese needs constant care and maintenance — a task which the Principal sees as crucial to the Aston vision. This network is better serviced now because of the purchase of a word-processor which enables so much more to be done with the material produced by the staff. On the broader front, the rewriting of the handbook and publicity materials has proved an important step on this road and it was helpful that skilled students worked on the design and layout of this material so that the final products fitted the market for which they were intended.

II   THE PASTORAL TUTORS

In choosing a Pastoral Tutor, the Principal and diocese will be looking for someone of experience who lives within easy reach of the student and who is prepared to commit at least two hours per month to meeting with the student during the two years of the Aston Course. In making their choice consideration is paid to the student's particular needs, background, experience and strengths, and the scheme tries to find the Tutor who has the skill and patience to explore with the student the implications of all these things for the student's future vocation in God's world.

The scheme makes many great demands upon the student and constantly feeds in new input by means of the course-work, the Weekends, the Project Weeks and Summer School experiences. For the student to gain fully from these often challenging opportunities he or she must rely upon the Pastoral Tutor so that the input can be rightly understood, properly criticised and inwardly digested. The hope is for real change and substantial growth, so the Pastoral Tutor is asked to support and challenge the student at depth over the two crucial years in their journey of faith with the scheme.

During these years, students often need to make very critical decisions, sometimes about family, housing, employment, vocation, the parish and so on. As well as acting as a sounding board so that the student can make well-considered decisions, the Pastoral Tutor has to encourage the student to become more aware of the dynamics of decision-making, attitudes to authority, and responsibility, as they are experienced.

The student's prayer life and spiritual development need all the support the Pastoral Tutor is able to offer. In the initial period of membership, particularly, the student has to adjust to increased demands on his or her time and energy, and frequently old patterns of life style, prayer and devotion are no longer found to be appropriate. As maturity increases, earlier forms of spirituality and daily routine may be seen as inadequate and new approaches are often discovered through the conversations.

The Pastoral Tutor must always be aware of the wider context of the student's life and to that end is asked to meet with students and families wherever this is possible. Students who are in paid employment often invite the Pastoral Tutor to attend at their work-place when it is possible, and those students who are unemployed usually have a great wealth of experience to share with the Tutor.

Tutors are chosen from an extraordinarily broad pool of willing volunteers, lay and ordained, and play a crucial role in broadening the students' experience and giving them opportunity for personal growth and spiritual maturation. They often turn out to be long-term friends and mentors well after the end of the student's Aston Course. The Pastoral Tutors' reports are given considerable weight during the Aston assessment process because of the depth and significance of the relationship which develops during the two years. The assessment process will be described more fully in the next chapter.

III THE FIRST YEAR STUDY COURSES

The study courses are an integral part of the overall programme and must cater for a student body which includes graduates, some in arts or theology, as well as those who have had no formal education since they left school. It has therefore been important to offer a whole battery of courses at different levels and in various areas depending upon the individual needs of each student. This has taken years to achieve and is still in process of development.

Even before the student formally registers, during the early induction process, there are now specifically written courses of study on offer. Geoff Milsom has been instrumental in the production of these preliminary courses, bringing with him many years' experience of working with our students when Aston still bought in its courses from external educational agencies.

The Preliminary Course is optional and can be taken at any pace by those students who have been through the early stages of Aston's induction process but who have yet to begin the course in earnest. Out of some forty to forty-five students who start the scheme each year, three-quarters will make some use of the Preliminary Course. It is attractively produced and starts with a 'Hello' chapter from the writer, The style is down to earth, hopefully non-threatening, and informative for those who are not used to study as well as for those who could do with a glance back to check that over their academic years they have not fallen into too many bad study-habits. The course begins like this:

I am writing the opening paragraphs of this section of the course seated at a rectangular oak Victorian dining table in a room in which my two boys, aged five and eleven respectively, frequently play. It is a through room from the front hall to the kitchen. At present, the boys having recently gone to bed, it is quiet. My wife is drying her hair in the bedroom and the cat is asleep by the gas fire. Upstairs I have a study which has a large desk, many bookshelves and all the reference works I shall need to write this course; and you will no doubt wonder why I work at the dining room table. Well, that's a hard one to answer because basically it's all tied up with the sort of person I am. True, I do mutter in non-standard English when I can't remember the details of a reference and have to run upstairs to look it up, but generally I feel far easier working at the dining table than my office desk.

Having admitted all this, I have given you some pointers already to the most important lesson you need to learn at this early stage. If you wish to make the most of your study periods you need to experiment; principally with places and times.

So the Preliminary Course begins with the situation of the student, trying to get study time sorted out and a suitable environment for it, yet all the time stressing that the only 'right' way is what is right for that particular individual. The Tutor speaks directly to the student through the pages, setting exercises to do on the spot, as well as longer assignments which can be sent in to be marked and commented upon. The learning is put very much into the student's hands and this is an important part of the Aston vision—that as an adult the student remains in control of her or his learning. This point is one of the educational axioms which arise out of the theology behind the course and in turn feed the theological experiences of the student.

The Preliminary Course takes intending students through the basic questions of how to timetable and budget time to allow for all the new elements to be covered, without squeezing out time for family, chores, prayer and recreation. The chapters on how to set about writing essays and on reading skills are always welcomed by students, and even graduates complain that if they had known this years ago life would have been so much easier!

Having produced the Preliminary Course, Geoff Milsom and the staff team went to work on producing a course of study to take students through the first six months of the Aston Scheme proper. It was felt by all to be important that all students start off with the same material so as to help towards the cohesion of each student intake year, but because of the tremendous spread of background and previous experience within the student body the course had to be written to allow for extraordinary flexibility within it. The resulting course, 'New Dimensions', consists of eight units all loosely linked to the theme 'The Individual in Society'. Each unit approaches a different aspect of this theme, attempting to introduce students to a variety of disciplines and sound argument. It includes many elements which were specifically requested by former students and is designed to take students from where they are to the point where they can effectively tackle study material at university foundation course level. In this it seems to be proving very successful. The course comprises eight units of work to do at home, but, as each area is focused, a corresponding residential weekend attempts to cover similar ground by using more experiential methods. The introductory page of 'New Dimensions' sets out the unit topics as follows:

Unit One. 'Childhood Experiences'
An introduction to the working of the child's mind through the writings of novelists, poets, theologians, psychologists and philosophers. The aim is to

demonstrate how early experiences affect the adult personality. There is also opportunity for some to consider adolescent experience similarly in this unit.

Unit Two. 'The Roles We Play in Our Groups'

A look at ourselves and the various groups with which we have contact. Passages from recent novels and pieces specifically written for the course will form the spine of this particular study which will aim to demonstrate the importance of the individual's contact with others.

Unit Three. 'Looking at Society'

A brief look at how society functions, concentrating particularly upon British Society and the groups and sub-cultures within it, in order that we may further appreciate the factors that make us what we are.

Unit Four. 'Where Do I Fit In?'

A more detailed study of a novel, *The Plague* by Albert Camus. Set in Oran, North Africa, the story details the life of a town shut off from the outside world because of bubonic plague. How the characters interact may help us to understand ourselves and others a little better.

Unit Five. 'What's Around Me Now?'

A community project in which students will be assisted in the production of an in-depth consideration of their own area, town, village or street.

Unit Six. 'Anglicanism'

Just as the society to which we belong is an amalgam of many different types of people, so our Church has developed from many different traditions. Just as within our society we expect acceptance of the foibles of our own character, so within our Church we must learn to respect the traditions of others. This unit will help students to understand these varying traditions and groupings and why we belong to them.

One of the assignments for this unit includes a visit by the student to an unfamiliar church.

Unit Seven. 'What Does the Artist Offer?'

At its core, the basic question of this unit is 'What is the function of the Artist in Society?' Beyond that, we attempt to introduce students to the technicalities involved in the study of art, music and literature.

Unit Eight. 'How Can We Speak of God?'

There are two sections of this unit. The first considers how we try to put our thoughts about God into words and asks the question 'What is Theology?' In the second section, we look at how we use language and what happens when religion goes further than our language can cope with. 'Language at the Limits.'

Alongside this New Dimensions' course the student is expected to talk out the more personal implications of the material with his or her Pastoral Tutor and staff, and many of the thorny social and theological issues raised by the material are grappled with at the corresponding residential weekends. The whole approach of New Dimensions is captured in its title — to take a fresh look at what is familiar, to capture a new dimension on something and investigate it from a variety of angles. The combination of familiarity and newness is very important in affirming the value of the students' past experience and encouraging them to explore further. This ties in with the nature of the residential weekends, for it is here that a change has occurred. Now they are times of affirmation and learning because an atmosphere of trust and support is created at the beginning. It then becomes possible to challenge students to develop when they already feel valuable as individuals, much preferable to the opposite educational mode of destruction and rebuilding which leaves the student out of control of his or her own learning and ready to be shaped by someone else who holds the power. This destruction model is far from the Aston vision of affirmation and challenge because it fails ultimately to affirm the value of the adult in theology or education and is very questionable in terms of its theology of power and authority.

After six months the students are well prepared to embark upon a course of intensive study with the Open University. Most students will choose to undertake a foundation course in the Arts or the Social Sciences and some will be ready to be stretched even further by an advanced level course selected from the hundreds on offer. Among the many advantages of using an Open University course at this stage in the programme is the fact that the OU already has a nationwide network of seminar groups clustered around very able tutors skilled in adult education. It also gives students a chance to work in secular seminar groups where they can learn to argue their case in the cut and thrust of debate but with the support of Aston experience and staff backing them up from outside. The OU also provides an objective non-church standard by which students can assess their progress, and this usually proves very positive. Last year we were able to boast of a 100 per cent pass rate amongst our students taking OU courses. Another interesting spin-off from using OU courses is that it allows our students to become even more aware of the tendency in England for scholarship to be in the hands of the middle class. The raising of this consciousness *before* Theological College allows our students to engage with the personal implications of this and work out appropriate strategies to deal with it.

IV THE RESIDENTIAL EXPERIENCES

We have already described how some forty to forty-five prospective students are inducted each year in a non-threatening and developmental way by coming first to a small Induction Day, then by having a visit to their home environment area by the Principal. They next attend a Saturday session where they meet and work with half their student colleagues. It is not until their first weekend together that they have to cope with meeting all their own year at one time. This gradual build-up is found to be valuable in not overwhelming a new student and thus it enables him or her to be themselves in a largely non-threatening environment while constantly learning new things about themselves and others.

The planning of a residential weekend is a complex process. The Principal invites two or three of the voluntary staff-team to come together with the full time staff for a day to do the planning. The first task the planning team undertakes is to share one with another their own inner emotions and present circumstances. Only when this has been properly heard can the next part of the group process be adequately engaged, for only then will they be able to discuss sensitively where they feel the particular students, and families who will be attending the weekend in question, are up to and what their pressing needs might be. These will form the agenda for the weekend. A great deal of time is then spent in stating the theme and the precise aim and intention of the event. It is usually not until the afternoon of any planning day that the individual sessions and methods to be used at the event are discussed and clarified. Methods will therefore vary enormously depending upon the aim of the weekend and the distinct purpose of each session within the overall process. Role play, video, group work, simulation, Bible study, practicals, worship and prayer, lecturettes, buzz groups, paints, drama, sculpture, informal meeting and much more will form the content of weekends, depending upon what is appropriate to the needs of the students.

The emphasis, then, is clearly upon experiential engagement with the issue in question at any Aston educational event, and this is to allow space and opportunity for the student to discover something for him or her self and to make connections with previous pieces of learning and experience.

This approach places the learner in the centre — it is subjective in the full sense of the word — and it does not shrink from that, for discovered knowledge is better learned and more highly prized by a student than knowledge fed in by another person on the didactic approach. The debate between didactic and experiential education is essentially engaged in the questions of power and who wields it, and of whether theology is 'made' or 'handed on'. Despite using some lecturing in the second year (partly to prepare students for the dominant method still used in colleges) the Aston Scheme goes for the experiential method at its residential events, seeing it as a much valued method in its attempt to get right theologically and educationally. The dialogical mode of education, which is found in experiential education and not in didactic education, recognises as its theological basis the God who calls to Adam and asks him a question, the God who in Jesus questions those who want to find the truth, and it starts by accepting the particular 'incarnation' of the students. In dialogical education the learner dialogues both with the material, questioning it and allowing it to question her or him, as well as with other learners and teachers. The process is essentially dynamic, creating a spiral of experiences and learning and not what has been called the 'front end loading view of education'.

If you are reading this description alongside the flow diagram 3 on page 48 you will see there that among the themes covered on the Aston weekends there will be 'Who am I?', 'Ministry in Context', 'Spirituality', 'Joy and Sorrow', 'What is Theology?' and 'The Nature of the Church'. Within these themes there will be covered the central issues of ethnicity, gender and class and no student will be allowed to side-step these questions since they are the basic areas of concern for today's society. But whatever the concern or theme, the event will be designed to 'touch' the student at many levels so that change in attitude, understanding and behaviour can result as appropriate.

The Summer Schools are also planned to run experientially but with much more time available and with very large numbers attending, these carefully organised educational and recreational events have to be experienced to be believed. A major theme, such as 'Exodus', 'Kingdom', 'Eternal Life' or 'Church', is engaged by means of an experientially designed process culminating in some great events to express the learning of the week. Including professionally run crèche facilities for children and provision for the inclusion of students' partners in all events where they wish to join, the Aston Summer School will cater for some two hundred or more participants.

This integrated admixture of distance learning study courses and experiential residential events seeks to provide an educational package which fulfils in some measure the overall Aston educational aims, which might be related thus:

1 To promote a dialogical mode of education so that all participants may grow in freedom and fulfilment and discern their mission.

2 To help students integrate learning by an action-reflection-action process.

3 To provide students with skills required to investigate our traditions.

4 To promote self-confidence in study and the life of faith.

5 To enable students to experience theology as an active and critical reflection.

6 To help students affirm the various ministries in God's church and discern their own.

7 To empower some students to go on to Theological Colleges ready to use that experience to the full.

8 To encourage the students to understand themselves better as persons and Christians.

V   THE ASTON ASSESSMENT PROCESS

Over the ten years of Aston's life the rigorous self-assessment process for which it has become well known has been developing and improving. It will be described in proper detail in Chapter 4, but here we must make it crystal clear that the Aston self-assessment process will be entirely misunderstood if it is plucked from its context within the overall two-year process of the syllabus. Indeed this has been known to be the case, as for example when a student once shared an Aston assessment report with an interested friend who totally misunderstood the nature of that report and the framework within which it was set.

It must be remembered that some Aston students start their course from a very low state of morale. When the Principal makes his first visit to the intending student he is often assailed by anger, frustration and hurt at being told by the Church to undertake what will amount to an extra two years of ministerial training. Some feel that Aston is reserved only for sub-standard candidates and indeed sometimes Church officials will encourage the candidate to think and feel this way. The Principal has to bear the brunt of this anger and is often told by intending students that 'everything about Aston stinks', 'this decision does not come from God and I am going to get it changed', or 'when I saw that there was not much Greek in the syllabus I knew your course was cr___'. It is therefore all the more astounding that by the end of their first year nearly all students are singing the praises of the scheme. The change seems to occur at around the time of the mid-term self-assessment, for it is then that the student sees that it is his or her own concerns and issues around which the whole syllabus clusters. 'It wasn't until I came to that assessment halfway through the course that I began to make proper sense of the syllabus and what it was doing for me.'

The complex process of letter and report writing, with the responses and observations, which comprises the first assessment takes place towards the end of the first year and right through the first Summer School. Only after the first weekend of their second year do students begin to perceive how very far they have come on their personal journey; they have begun to formulate clearly what major issues now confront them in their ministerial and personal formation. The second year syllabus is then flexibly geared around the issues which have emerged from this first self-assessment process.

VI   THE SECOND YEAR SYLLABUS

The second year syllabus is designed to climax in a presentation by each student of an in depth project study of a theme that they have themselves specified, derived from the issues which have surfaced for them during the mid-term self-assessment process.

Into this project each student is expected to build proper biblical reflection, and the second year syllabus therefore begins with a course of introduction to Bible scholarship. Aston was helped in the preparation of this course by the Reverend Dr Philip Cliff, one-time Director of the Department of Church Education at Westhill College, Birmingham. He personally introduces the course to the students at a residential weekend event and explains how biblical scholarship has come a long way since its over-indulgence in destructive criticism. The course is based on the books *How to Read the New Testament* and *How to Read the Old Testament* by Charpentier (SCM Press). Whilst giving students opportunity to acquaint themselves with the biblical text, this introduces them to the realisation that a vast oral tradition and a worshipping and witnessing community stand behind the text as it comes to us. Students are helped to use the tools of scholarship to reach back behind the text to the experiences that engendered it and then to utilise that learning and their discoveries in their own developing devotional life. Students study the New Testament first and then look at the Hebrew Scriptures in order to see how Jesus was influenced by that context. The whole emphasis is, in this way, upon scholarly *use* of the Bible rather than critique of the text, which is part of the theological task which will be better accomplished later at Theological College or Course.

As the student becomes more able to bring biblical insight to his or her concerns, so also it is expected that it will inform the parish work experience in which he or she is engaged. They are therefore required during this period to work locally under the supervision of the incumbent to acquire the experience of parochial visiting and preaching. This all helps to locate the student and use his or her parochial roots. Soon after this a short course based upon the disciplines of the social sciences is undertaken so that the locality may be more clearly understood and the issues of our day more crisply focused.

Throughout this period the student has been working with the Pastoral Tutor and staff to formulate the theme for his or her Aston Project, which then becomes the prime focus of attention for the remainder of the scheme's programme.

VII   THE ASTON PROJECT

The project is a self-directed, multi-disciplinary study investigating a theme in which the students have a personal investment. They are encouraged to use themes arising out of their assessment experience and to bring these to a project week in the February of their second year. Project weeks are run for only twelve students at a time with a high staff-student ratio. (With the increasing student numbers on Aston, these weeks are a good method of recapturing the intimacy of Aston's earlier years.) At the week, each student belongs to an even more closely knit group composed of only four students and a Project Tutor, where they are helped, through the group process, to arrive at a realistic project with specified aim, objectives and methodology. During the week there are also exercises in 'doing theological reflection' and the group experiences and 'games' are used to develop awareness and skills in leadership and group work. One requirement of the project is that the student has to create and enable a house group for about five meetings on the theme of the project and then write up the learning (both content and process) of the group. Each student has a Project Consultant appointed in their home area whom they can use as a resource and enabler of more critical reflection. Book reviews, interviews, Bible studies, visits and fieldwork are all written up in appendices and the major essay component of the project addresses the aim and objectives and concludes with a clear statement of what the student has learned for the future, especially as it relates to their vocational journey. Written material, videos and tapes, tapestry or dance, etc., can be used in the presentation of the project, which takes place at the students' final Summer School.

Obviously the aim of a project is to learn about the chosen theme and to gain insight into particular problems, but working through the project involves the development of a number of essential ministerial skills. It involves learning how to structure and manage group activity, how to negotiate between one group and another, how to balance the pressure to complete a task and maintain a group. It demands that the student train and work with and alongside layfolk and engage in the theological enterprise in a non-competitive co-operative manner. The production of the project makes concerted academic demands upon the student, while the presentation of it asks the student to recognise the needs for basic design and PR skills in modern ministry. When the projects are appraised, staff and tutors want to be sure that the students have been able to specify the aim and work to the programme and objectives they have set for themselves. They will want to see evidence of the application to the theme of what they have been learning throughout the course and a worthy attempt at biblical and theological reflection and critique of the theme.

So far project themes have included the following:

Risks in the Pastoral Ministry
Resourcing the Rural Church
Giving and Receiving Empathy
The Christian Isolated at Work
Sexism and its Effect on Women's Ministry
Working Class Gifts in the Church of England
Church and Community in the Inner City
Dignity and Worth in the World of Unemployment

At the End of the Course

Towards the end of the Aston programme the Aston Assessors make their recommendation to the student's sponsoring bishop, who then determines whether she or he should go on to College or Course or be helped to understand their vocation in some other way. If they have completed the study aspects of the programme satisfactorily they will be awarded the Aston Certificate of Studies which is now accredited by ACCM. The certificate may seem unimportant in itself to those who already have many such pieces of paper, but the power of affirmation that such a certificate carries for people with no previous qualifications makes it an important element in the scheme's provision, especially for those who are asked to continue in 'non-accredited' lay ministry having undertaken this very rigorous programme of training.

The Aston Course now ends in time for all students to prepare themselves to go on to College. Aston attempts to work hand in glove with the Colleges and Courses in order that students' transfers may be as painless and as productive as possible for the student.

The scheme has sent students on to all the Theological Colleges of England and to some Diocesan Ministerial Training Courses as well. The Principal sends a letter to the appropriate College or Course explaining where the student is up to in his or her vocational journey and training. The letter does not give all past details since these are not relevant to the student's present position. The Colleges' attitude is usually that ex-Aston students make interesting people to teach. The scheme attempts to find out what the Colleges are wanting so that it can help the student prepare accordingly. For example, nearly all Colleges use the lecturing style to a considerable extent, and so, although it is not part of Aston's teaching style, the staff prepare students to learn how to take lecture notes. Aston helps students to learn the variety of reading skills necessary for academic work and has proved to be very good at this. The scheme aims to prepare the students for College so that they can use the opportunity it presents. Aston students are skilled at handling academic material and at discerning what is important and what is not. They are able to bring their experience to bear on issues and their theology to bear on what is going on around and within them.

Every year there will be many non-graduates on the Aston Scheme and some of them will so blossom academically that it will be proper for them to read for a degree at College, even though they would never have dreamt of such a thing just two years before.

Because of the complete flexibility of the new Aston syllabus, it is possible to prepare some students for special university entrance examinations or matriculation to make degree programme entry possible.

All students are given help emotionally to make the move to College, and matters of class or cultural rooting, domestic anxiety and study nerves are given proper place towards the end of the course. Likewise, in the more academic matters, the basic elements of New Testament Greek are introduced to students and help is given with the reading lists which Colleges provide to their intending students, all so that the transition may be made smoothly.

The Staff Team

As well as the large team of local Academic and Pastoral Tutors the scheme has the assistance of those who volunteer as Project Tutors and those who help to run the experiential Weekends and Summer Schools. In addition, specialists are brought in from time to time to help run extra courses in study skills and to assist in specialist counselling. It is for the central full time staff to co-ordinate this network and they in turn are assisted by work consultants and a group process consultant.

The quality of the Project Tutors and the Weekend and Summer School staff is crucial to the proper implementation of the Aston vision. The team has a good broad representation of churchmanship giving all the students at least one person to identify with. The students also receive from the assistant staff a wide and representative cross-section of models of ministry. There is continuity, with each member of the assistant staff team appearing about twice a year, and there is also change, since new members are added from time to time. There is a clear black voice and strong inner city and rural voices. The issue of women's ministry is one that is coming more to the fore. There is pain in working with women who know themselves to be in a minority and who are unsure what the Church is saying to them about their gender. The women on the staff team have been brought in for reasons apart from gender, with an attempt to avoid both tokenism and also any labelling as feminist with consequent deriding of the whole issue by some of the students. That this is the case makes it imperative that the move for inclusive language, and so on, comes equally from the men in the staff team as from the women.

Questions of class and of ethnicity receive equal prominence in order that students learn to value themselves properly and to value the special gifts and experiences of others. To this the staff team are expected to bring special awareness and sensitivity. The vulnerability and openness of the staff to the students is very important, and so not only the choice of them but also their maintenance within the team is vital. This is especially the case during the Summer Schools when they are giving out all the time. It is the job of the Principal to enable the other staff members to remain open and to keep growing just as the students are expected to do. To this end a great deal of personal trust and sharing has to go on at all levels and it is one of the blessings of the scheme that an atmosphere and ethos are engendered and maintained wherein this quality of relationship is made possible.

The weight of staff work falls of course mainly upon the four full time staff members, the Administrator, the Adult Educationalist, the Vice-Principal and the Principal, who seek themselves to maintain their own development by means of self-assessment and mutual work appraisal. This mirrors the very thorough self-assessment process in which the Aston students engage and to which we now turn in detail.

4

TESTING VOCATION

Who am I? Who is this person named Mark or Mary whom God calls? I guess that is for most of us a daunting yet exciting question. Our response is always that of a person on a journey, to whom our past, present and anticipated future all contribute. We are always in a state of becoming, we've never arrived.

To respond to that question knowing that others are going to communicate how they perceive me seems even more daunting. Yet such is the way that on Aston we seek greater awareness of ourselves as children of God, called by him into Christian ministry. That call we share with all Christians, but every one is a unique person and every Christian has a unique calling. Those who come on Aston are all pursuing what they perceive in different ways as a call or vocation to full time ordained or lay ministry. To test that particular vocation is the essential purpose of the Aston assessment process.

'Who am it?' became the in-joke among one year group of Aston students after a typing slip on one weekend programme printed 'it' for 'I'. The experience can feel at times as though you are a piece of dough and everybody has a go at bashing it. Yet we are never 'it', we are created to be responsible for our own lives, and only the person in question can really make use of the perceptions of others about them. This is why each individual starts off the process of assessment by drawing together much personal reflection over the year in a self-assessment letter.

We are going to listen in on the assessment process through the experience of four students who have given permission for extracts from their assessment letters and reports to be quoted. All we have done is to substitute other names.

After about nine months on Aston, Jennifer and Colin receive a letter from the Principal asking them to prepare and write a mid-term self-assessment letter. The Principal's letter contains the following:

> I know that this is a very demanding matter and will require of you much time and prayerful examination. Be assured that you are not alone in this and that you will be very much in our prayers these next few months . . .

65

Self-assessment in Aston has two aims:

a. The first aim is to help you find out more about yourself; what your own strengths and hopes are, what your needs in training now are and what God's purpose is for you.

b. The second aim is for you to help the Assessors in making their assessment of your progress in Aston thus far.

The letter continues with two pages of guidance on self-assessment — guidance which has grown more detailed over the years.

Jennifer's Story

We grew up partly in council estates, some with great neighbourliness. Later we moved to the countryside . . . as we grew up Dad had some periods of unemployment.

We were encouraged to value the family unit. However, part of me tends to be 'over-independent'. Through a period of loneliness, I have begun to believe it is good to nourish one or two close friendships as well as having a wide circle. Through work and life experience, I have been learning a 'letting go' process. Through growing up, and broken relationships, I can appreciate the effects of our past, but live for today. This can be liberating.

Both life and my psychiatric nursing teach me about my own reaction to situations. I am slowly learning to differentiate between my own feelings and those of others. I do find confrontation, anger and resentment difficult to absorb. I became alert spiritually through a gracious experience of our Lord. But there have been and continue so, many struggles along the way; for instance, sometimes doubting God's loving kindness. Recently my faith felt as if it were in a void or darkness. It seemed to continue for ever. Through it I found some healing, and became a wee bit more patient . . . I think the whole experience is one I will sometimes struggle with. And I suspect it is related to my pride too.

When I first realised I was to undertake the Aston Scheme, I was afraid. There was a tension between feeling called to go ahead yet believing I would never cope with work, people and study. The first few weekends I was nervous.

Some of the areas we look at are painful, but I welcome it if it means we grapple with more important issues . . . I am not always able to verbalise what I am feeling, but need to reflect. I am learning a little about the suffering Jesus identifying with people in their pain. But I know somewhere we have to proclaim the resurrection into a 'hopeless' situation.

My own self-perception is that I am a paradox. I enjoy solitude, yet love being with people. I can appear to be disorganised yet need order. I find it difficult to accept or receive, I can be easily distracted, or have poor concentration. Yet I will ponder something for ages. Sometimes I take life too seriously, yet see funny aspects to most situations. I sometimes try to justify mistakes, instead of being gracious. I like making people laugh and affirming people's worth. I am perceptive at times, and have an enquiring mind. I hope to become more relaxed, and more compassionate in the future.

Vocationally, I am unable to be dogmatic, but being a full time worker in the Church of England is the one service which consistently appeals. Yet I realise more and more that it is a difficult task. I therefore feel inadequate at times . . .

The staff report that Jennifer received contained the following:

Jennifer is a warm, sympathetic and inspiring person who as yet does not seem to appreciate her own gifts and potential. She has a breadth of personal and social experience upon which she reflects with perception and sensitivity. Jennifer has a strong sense of the suffering world and is committed to respond to Christ's yearning to serve that world through his people. Yet, despite all this, she retains a timidity and a lack of self-confidence which is particularly manifested in larger group work.

She has been concerned about her academic ability and her tutors have noted the difficulty she has with written expression, and yet when writing hastily on a train journey about her spiritual experiences of life, she shows a real potential for a moving and descriptive style of wonderfully lucid and penetrating expressiveness. Perhaps when she is relaxed her best gifts come to the fore.

One senses the making of a good pastor in Jennifer which is enhanced by her professional training and experience in this field. She is aware of some of the early experience and other reasons for her own lack of self-confidence and we trust that she will continue to explore these factors in her pastoral tutorials. She does still show a little evidence of fear of rejection but is becoming much more confident in the one-to-one relationship, where she excels . . . there is still some fuzziness about Deaconess Orders in her mind, which is very understandable . . .

We believe that Jennifer has it in her to perform an important prophetic role in ministry, although we doubt whether she would as yet acknowledge that . . .

Jennifer is asked to acknowledge and respond to the staff report, which she does as follows:

Thank you for your report. I have read it several times now! In doing so I found it helpful in discovering more about myself. And relating that to what sort of ministry would be possible for me.

I am uncertain as to why I find it difficult to speak in large groups, when I was in my early teens I tended to be the opposite! However, I do agree that I need to 'risk myself', and hope to have the courage so to do.

With regard to the 'fuzziness about Deaconess Orders', in truth, it has been partly because I was curious about Holy Orders or the 'Religious Life'.

But, having thought this through a little more, I feel I would be better suited to the work of a Deaconess. If the opportunity for Pastoral Assistant's work does transpire, I also hope this will enlighten me further.

I am unable to acknowledge regarding 'prophetic role in ministry' because I would wish to clarify what you mean by the terminology! But not because I would not wish to partake in it . . .

Jennifer's letter takes up the guidance that is given in the Principal's letter about writing the self-assessment as a journey and reflecting on all aspects of life, not just those of being an Aston student. The letter recommends that each person should look in particular at their personal development, their academic development, their spiritual/ vocational journey and their understanding of the world. They are asked to conclude the letter with some targets for the coming year.

There are major elements of the education programme that serve to help students with their self-assessment. The residential weekends and Summer Schools largely take the form of experiential learning, with growth in self-awareness that can sometimes be disturbing and painful. This requires the staff, full time and assistant, to share of themselves and their own vulnerabilities. Resources for ministry are seen to be derived from our weaknesses as well as from our strengths. It is helpful that there is space between such intense and often joyful events, for most learning comes through the reflection in between times and in the continuing relationships among family and friends, at work and in the local church.

Some reflective writing on such topics as 'My Journey — What God has meant to me' and on childhood, group and community experiences, helps in the discernment of 'Who I am'. The Pastoral Tutor relationship is concerned with helping students become aware of themselves and with their affirmation of themselves as human beings created in love by God — warts and all. Students are encouraged to discuss their own self-assessment letter with their Pastoral Tutors and the Pastoral Tutors are encouraged to share the content of the report they are writing at the same time about their relationship and their understanding of the students and their development needs. This is often an occasion for considerable opening up and deepening of the student/Pastoral Tutor relationship.

Colin's Story

As we listen to Colin's experience, we hear also the voice of the Pastoral Tutor. First, from Colin's own self-assessment:

68

It was four years ago practically to the day when I walked into a church for the first time in fourteen years . . . and . . . gave my life to Christ. My new life with Jesus asked me to rethink many things and called upon me to re-examine much that I had taken for granted . . . I offered myself for the ordained ministry. In the following few months, I learnt a number of things that were to slow me down and give me pause for consideration. It came as a shock to realise that I was considered by some to be abrasive, and often intolerant. It came as a bigger shock to realise these opinions weren't groundless. The world hadn't suddenly turned against me for, despite criticism, people were still supportive, both of me personally and of my vocation.

I have by inclination and by training a searching and questioning nature but this has not always led me to understanding, I think because I have usually employed it in a singular and isolated way. If I have needed an answer I have sought it by assuming black and white parameters and, as my tutor describes it, have gone straight for the jugular. It has led people to believe I am insensitive, unaware and often detached . . . I also felt that I had a great sense of love and caring, particularly for my family and close friends. I have, however, been guilty of a smothering restricting love that has hindered balanced relationships with those for whom I care.

The trouble with self-discovery is that you begin to perceive just how imperfect you are and were this not counterbalanced by the realisation that God's love can still handle it, then I suspect my stamina for the process would have failed me long since.

I . . . grow increasingly aware of injustice, unnecessary suffering and perhaps even a sense of hopelessness . . . what do I want to do about these things is a question which I ask myself at least once every day; its answer is inevitably tied up with my sense of vocation and the way I feel I am being changed and for what purposes. I feel a great need to get alongside those who do suffer and lack hope and I grow increasingly aware of my material wealth in a world of poverty. I am also aware that my vocation is not to be a social worker. I don't belittle that calling, nor do I undervalue it, but I know that this kind of work, even if it has the added dimension of Christian witness, is not that to which I am called. I believe I am being equipped for an ordained ministry that has as its priority the Gospel message and its proclamation, it is the building up of Christ's body in word and sacrament and guiding and assisting in its mission of care and concern that I see more fully my vocation to God's service. The more I am shown my inadequacy for this task, the more I am convinced of its truth, the vision for it has never dimmed and my confidence in God to bring it about has been nurtured by the fruits of putting my trust in him.'

Colin's Pastoral Tutor writes as follows:

. . .Colin, like the rest of us, is the product and to some extent the victim of a particular background. His upbringing and training have both given him a typical executive's approach to life. His instinct when presented with a new situation is to identify the problem and then produce a solution. In consequence, he is not naturally good at listening, and is inclined to weigh in too soon with action or the offer of good advice. In addition, he has what I should call an excessively intellectual approach to life — a mind that seeks to understand, and that expects always to find answers. I doubt therefore whether he always gives enough weight to his emotional perceptions... Colin is well aware of these parts of himself, and is sufficiently open to seek after a growth and widening of his approach to life . . .

An extract from the staff report about Colin reads:

Colin is able to name the insensitivity he showed towards . . .others when he first realised he should respond wholeheartedly to a new vocation. His managerial salesmanship Christianity would not have won as many hearts as he imagined it would and his 'tough-guy' bearing betrayed an inner lack of confidence and self-esteem.

. . .despite all the pitfalls which Colin has named, he really can be a joy to be with, a challenging presenter of God's Word and an inspiring encourager of the crestfallen. He is beginning too to talk of his own emotions much more genuinely and he is developing a proper anger at social injustice and a fervent desire to bring life's issues and the reality of Christ's love together into a life of service.

During Summer School, each student has an interview with the member of the team of Assessors with whom they had an interview at their first Aston weekend in the previous October. They will know that the Assessor has read their self-assessment letter, their Pastoral Tutor's letter, the staff report and their response — and occasionally comments from their vicar. Each student should have seen it all, for open relationships with the Pastoral Tutor and the staff are vital. Communicating the truth in love is at times a painful and risky business. The supportive as well as challenging nature of these relationships and of the student fellowship is essential. Colin writes with some reflections on the above process as follows:

Writing my self-assessment letter required a personal search to a depth I had not previously undertaken. It was an exacting task, emotions were stirred, pain was often present and feelings of being exposed and vulnerable were and to a degree still are present. The feelings of exposure and vulnerability seemed to stem from knowing that I was 'baring my soul' in letter form to some eight or nine people. I now feel however that it was more of an exposure of myself to myself though this was no less difficult an experience.

I had left myself with no place to hide, and though this may speak well for honesty, it left me needing to be assured that I was still loved. In my experience this love and care was abundant through my Pastoral Tutor, the staff, and I think most importantly from my fellow students.

At the Summer School, the team of Assessors tries to meet informally with all students so that they can share information about each student as a team. They then have a meeting to inform the staff about how they see each person's progress. After that, the staff write another letter to each student outlining how the Assessors are seeing their progress and stating any matter that the Assessors consider crucial for the next year.

We are only halfway through the assessment process and we move on to listen to the experiences of Simon and Daniel who have already journeyed on from Aston.

Simon's Story

Simon's first self-assessment letter was fairly brief and unrevealing:

> I will begin with my academic growth. I must say I feel much more at ease with the thought of studying now than when I first began on the Aston Training Scheme, although I still feel sad that I seem to spend all of my periods of study purely concerned with getting my next assignment finished . . .
>
> About thoughts of my felt vocation to the ordained priesthood – all I feel able to say is that at times when I do not want to be an ordained minister I still feel this is the task the Lord has set before me.
>
> All in all I think I must say that my Aston experience has been challenging and unsettling, but in hindsight I can see that this process will have, and indeed is having, many benefits in my ministry . . .

Simon's Pastoral Tutor writes:

> There are some very positive experiences that Simon has gained from the Aston Scheme, one of which is the change of surroundings and lifestyle. Although he still has a dislike of studying and finds that the Aston Scheme is not very helpful to him in this direction he does say that he has gained more self-confidence in the academic side of the course. I feel his main difficulty is allotting time to his studies . . .
>
> The problems he has discussed with me so far are mainly concerned with the Aston Training Scheme in general and his relationships with other members of the scheme. He is concerned that others and perhaps particularly members of the staff do not see him as welcoming to other members of his group. He feels that this is not altogether true and, surprising though it may seem, he says he is rather shy in the early stages of meeting and sharing closely with other people.

From the outset his feelings have been, and still are, that the Aston Scheme is something he must do to be ordained; so far it has been little help in supporting his vocation. When asked what good the scheme has done for him, he replied that it has rooted him even more in the Catholic tradition...

One hopes that as time goes on, Simon will become a little less dogmatic in his ideas of the Christian faith and Christian people.

The staff report includes the following:

Simon is starting to learn both to study and make more effort in uncongenial relationships despite an initial air of reluctance to learn.

There are, however, a number of things that stand in the way of his personal and academic learning. He displays a strange mixture of shyness and cockiness. We get the feeling that unless people acceptably conform to his pre-determined pattern, he leaves the making of a relationship to others and even presents himself as antagonistic to them. This gives the impression he does not readily trust people and that others have to work to earn his trust, which is not exactly living the Gospel. He seems to have a 'besieged mentality' at times, seeing himself as almost the sole representative of the truth and having to cap what others say rather than listen to them. We would see this as an insecurity within, that derives status from being different and over against.

Simon expressed clearly the self-sacrifice of the cross but needs to meditate on, and be imbued with, the reality of resurrection experience, with love casting out fear, insecurity and mistrust.

We see him as having a strong vocation and a determined acceptance of the yoke of Christ, but training in things he doesn't naturally want to do will come hard and he has to come to terms with being in a loving fellowship with the whole Church . . .

We would also like to say that we hope very much that he will continue to have a mind and will of his own, dedicated to Christ, so that all he learns will be re-expressed with his natural freshness, enthusiasm and critique.

Simon's reply is quoted in full:

I acknowledge receipt of your reply to my mid-term self-assessment letter. Hopefully I can learn from your comments.

After the Summer School and the meeting with the Assessors, the staff wrote to Simon as follows:

After careful deliberation, the Assessors told us that they felt you had the potential to be a good priest but there seemed to be an inner rage which could lead almost to the destruction of yourself and others rather than provide the passion for ministry, unless you came to understand it better and came to terms with it. At present, it seems to press you to make exceptionally high demands on yourself and yet at the same time to be over-dependent upon strong personalities to sort of 'break you'. In between, many ordinary folk are bewildered and unable to relate to you and to what is happening in your devotional life which at times doesn't seem to ring true with who you are.

After much wrestling with himself and with others, Simon changed his approach in a number of ways, including moving to live in a very different community and parish. Simon's new vicar writes this, eight months later:

> He had learnt so much from his previous community, but now the staff felt that he needed to be confronted by an environment which would challenge another side of his personality.
>
> This is a very different parish from . . .where Simon was working previously . . .he has adapted very well to it . . .I have received very pleasing comments on his pastoral work and in discussion with me he has shown evidence of pastoral sensitivity and real depth. . . .He is seen, not only as a 'nice chap' but as someone with something to contribute and a man who can support what he is saying.
>
> . . .I detect . . .a growing ability to think things through to the very best of his ability. He appears to be much more honest about himself, for example, his frank admission of loneliness while he was living in the curate's house . . . In short, in the months he has been here, he has learned a lot about himself and acknowledged his weaknesses and insecurities whereas in earlier days he may have stated a case more emphatically to avoid facing a possible 'grey area' or uncertainty in his mind.
>
> I have been able to trust Simon with many confidences and he has never broken any confidence and I regard him as utterly trustworthy and reliable. Nevertheless, there have been one or two instances where he has been a bit tactless.

Simon writes of himself in his second self-assessment some months later:

> I will begin my report with the topic of academics. I must admit passing the OU course last year has really given my confidence in my academical ability a great boost. Passing this course also made me realise the truth of others when they said of me 'He is quite capable — merely lazy.' This new confidence helped me very much in the biblical course . . .
>
> . . .I suffered very greatly from loneliness . . .
>
> . . .work in the parish . . .I have enjoyed very much and found it a real learning experience . . .
>
> The relationships that have been happening around me during Aston have been a source of joy to me, but more importantly I feel are the relationships that have happened within myself . . .I was told by a staff member to 'be a better parent to myself'. I didn't really understand what he

meant until the Project Week, when we briefly mentioned Transactional Analysis. With hindsight I think I can say I am now a more caring parent, setting my child more accessible and acceptable tasks and standards, and at the same time I feel I have become a more responsive child.

. . . meditations . . . I have gone virtually full swing and use a more Jesuit form of prayer — Prayer of awareness of oneself and praying the Bible — putting myself in the actual scene.

Looking back at last year's assessment, with your comments about expressing clearly the self-sacrifice of the cross — I must say I feel the resurrection has actually happened in my life.

The staff report in the second year, which was written to the Assessors and also sent to Simon, contains the following:

We've never really doubted the sincerity of Simon's vocation to the priesthood or the depth of his devotional commitment. But there have been a number of times when we've really sweated over whether Simon would get himself together in such a way as to be ready to go on to residential college after his two years on Aston. The breakthrough now is that he is beginning both to be able to assess himself and to have the confidence to let go of his at times arrogant dogmatism. Comparing this year's self-assessment letter with last year's demonstrates clearly the progress. This does not mean that the first year was a waste of time — far from it. The seeds of the last few months' developments were made through the down-to-earth ordered life of the first year parish . . . His story of the farewell given to him by his fellow staff at the home where he works sounded as if this was a real religious awareness of belonging.

. . . Simon's always likeable personality is increasingly being used as a channel for ministry, though he still needs to find the best channel for his radicalism — we don't want him to lose that fire. The barriers have begun to come down within Simon and in his relationships with others . . .

We think he is still very much at the beginning of the journey of discovering the appropriate authority from within himself to manage his own life under God and the Church.

From Theological College, Simon now writes to say:

I see the search for self-knowledge and knowledge of God as inseparable; the closer you come to one the closer to the other. This is a search that I believe all Christians should be involved in, especially those called to minister in the Church. I think if a person is not involved with continual self-assessment, their ability to give fully of themselves is hindered, if not removed.

Aston assessment is sometimes very painful, but in the end we reap the benefits 100-fold . . .

Daniel's Story

Great care is taken with the help of the diocese in matching each student with a personal Pastoral Tutor. A Pastoral Tutor needs to become a friend with whom the student can really share of themselves and needs to be secure enough him or herself to be able to challenge and speak the truth — or ask the incisive question — in love.

There is no work to be produced for the two-hour monthly meetings yet that is where the vital work of reflection and assessment goes on. This is where learning is really taken into oneself and even 'created'. That learning comes from reflection on the whole and the wholeness of life not just on the content of the training course. Daniel's story is a particular example of this. He writes as follows:

> The period I've spent as a member of the Aston Scheme has been one of change in so many areas. Perhaps the most significant, as I see it, is that of a greater self-awareness and self-acceptance on my part. Considering the questions 'Who am I?' and 'Why am I like I am?' has made me look very closely at myself, I think for the first time. I have become aware of the way in which my childhood experiences . . . have affected me. Within the past few weeks I have been able to accept the reality of my adoption . . . It is a great release to be able to accept this mysterious part of myself.
>
> My childhood made me repress, to a very large extent, feeling and emotions. I'm not the sort of person to do things on impulse; always weighing too carefully possible and sometimes impossible consequences . . . During the past year or so I've been able to express feelings more readily, and have begun to be somewhat less staid. I'm sure that my renewed interest in music and my recently starting to compose music is connected with this.
>
> Over recent months, I have felt that my relationship with Judith has become somehow more full and rounded, even though we've been married very happily for ten years. This may result from my growing awareness of the need to communicate about all aspects of our lives, especially about those things which we do separately.
>
> The past three months have been affected by my having been very ill with mumps and orchitis. I've been under considerable pressure at work for some time now due to a shortage of staff . . . I have learnt some things from my illness . . . I realised that I don't have to pretend to be a super spiritual giant — there will be failures, yet God loves me.

Brief comments from both his Pastoral Tutor and the staff report echo this. His Pastoral Tutor writes:

> . . . Daniel is in a very formative period. He has clearly developed a great deal over the last year as a person, and his consciousness of how he relates to

and fits in with other people, especially his own family, has expanded substantially. He knows this and rejoices in it. We have discussed his parental background, and this has been a useful if not easy process for him.

The staff report includes the following:

Some very profound things have been happening for Daniel over this past year. He arrived with us very urgently earnest and somewhat austere of temperament. He seemed to have closed himself off to his own emotional depths, and he and Judith were very dubious about what the Church wanted to 'do to them' in order that they should fit the middle-class ministry stereotypes. How different it all seems now. Daniel's letter moves through the story and the issues very well.

His serious bout of illness has made him address his tendency to be over-earnest and super-efficient for God . . . Daniel must relax much more and be accepting of his humanity, his drives, his gifts and limitations. He should be proud that God has created him as his son.

During the second year, Daniel's trials continued with his wife being seriously ill and with their premature baby's struggle to live. Just a few sentences from his second year self-assessment letter:

I think I have come into a more real and honest relationship with God. It seems as though many things have been forced away over the past two or so years and I am left having to own up to the real me before God.

I am still certain that God is calling me to the full time ordained ministry, although this calling must continue to be tested. Many things have fitted together to make me feel that the next stage should be our moving... to begin full time training.

His Pastoral Tutor wrote:

Thank you for your letter asking for an assessment on the pastoral relationship which I have enjoyed with Daniel over the last eighteen months or so. It has been a very fruitful exchange and I am glad to say that many of the processes of growth which I identified in the mid-term assessment have continued over the last twelve months. He has become a thoughtful, intuitive sort of person and with a growing self-awareness . . . I have been impressed with the way that he has coped with the various pressures and demands which have, of necessity, come to him. He has demonstrated courage and also an appropriate sympathy for others.

For Daniel, his personal and family experiences, but also work and church experiences, were the main channels for his formation. The staff report includes:

Daniel has experienced two years of hard testing and has proved to be honest, patient and strong.

Through his experience at Church and at work, Daniel has developed even more his capacity to absorb conflict and gently effect change, which indicates he will become a priest of considerable stature. Daniel's own thinking demonstrates clarity and pastoral sensitivity, but he also wisely checks out his thoughts about major decisions with others.

Daniel's vocation has become clearer as his appreciation of himself, his gifts, strengths and weaknesses and his understanding of the Church have broadened and deepened.

Daniel writes a year later about his experience as follows:

The Aston assessment process was for me a very formative period. Not in the sense that anything was forced on me but that I had to reflect honestly on myself—strengths, weaknesses, failures and successes. The tremendous thing was that this experience was guided by such sensitive and loving people; for facing up to ourselves as we are can be a shattering and painful experience. The process has stayed with me in that I feel able realistically to examine 'where I am' . . . I am extremely grateful for the Aston assessment procedure—it was a privileged experience . . .

Ministerial Formation

It will be apparent that the assessment process is at the heart of much of the learning and the ministerial formation on Aston, for it enables people to continue and even quicken their individual vocational journey. It helps in the following ways:

(i) It provides a very helpful and important drive towards self-awareness, personal development and openness to the love of God in our lives. As we listen to our lives and reflect with our eyes on Jesus Christ, we meet our creator and redeemer God who calls us to some particular and unique work for him.

(ii) It helps to direct the whole education process as students assess and identify their own growth needs and take charge of their own learning. This culminates (as described in Chapter 3) in students drawing up their own study project to pursue academically and personally some needs that they have identified in the assessment process.

(iii) It provides an experience of very open pastoral relationships which contributes to their own formation as pastors. This is primarily through the Pastoral Tutor relationship but all staff as well as students have to be prepared to be open. Daniel, in writing to comment on his time on Aston, says, 'You asked what makes Aston what it is . . . I think it is because both staff and students have to give of themselves to one another.'

(iv) It provides a training in assessment and priority setting which is an essential skill in the practice of ministry and for continuing ministerial education.

None of this is to suggest that vocation is just a question of personal awareness or of individual discovery. God calls us for and through his Church. Others have a key role to play in any assessment process and a decisive role in affirming our continuing training or our particular ministry, whether ordained or lay. Within our Church, the Bishop is the focus for that responsibility. The Assessors appointed by ACCM, who read all the assessment correspondence and meet a student over three residential occasions during the two years, make a recommendation to their Bishop about further training. Thus, Daniel received a letter from his Bishop which included:

> This letter confirms the telephone message which you will have received from me today. I am very pleased to be able to tell you that the Aston Assessors have recommended that you should proceed to further training (two years in residence) on completion of the Aston course in July. The way is now open to you to take the next step in your preparation for ordination. It has not been an easy time for you and we are all impressed at the way in which you have faced the challenge . . . I am sure you will now be able to benefit very considerably from the training upon which you are now embarking.

However caring the process of assessment, it inevitably involves risk as it is run for fallible human beings by fallible human beings. It can be very tough. It is important to quote from some of those who were more aware of the pain and difficulty. Again we quote with permission.

A student (1980-82) makes the following comments:

> During my time on the scheme, I think my biggest criticism is that of assessment. There was insufficient information given to the student regarding what was expected of him or even what the areas of required growth were. Different things seemed more important than others for different people which I am sure led to feelings of 'double standards'. Secrecy also surrounded the final assessment and some students were prevented from going to College for totally unknown reasons or at least vague reasons. I think it right that you ask those people for their reflections to try and see if the form of assessment did attempt to fulfil God's will for those people.

Part of the response to this criticism has been that, in recent years, the information and guidance given to students about the assessment process has increased greatly, and staff and Assessors try to make any particular concerns and doubts very clear during the two years rather than at the end. However, bearing such doubts and concerns is not always a simple matter. Also we are involved in an understanding of assessment which is not about reaching a specific standard but about becoming the unique person God intends. Another student (1983-85) writes:

> I thought I had to do Aston because ACCM felt I didn't fit the normal pattern for a C of E priest and that Aston was a means of fitting me into the mould. In fact, the reverse happened as I discovered my true unique individuality.

Another (1982-84) suggests this process can be too cosseting:

> I have always felt, however, there to be a certain ambiguity between the Christian need to die to self and the length of time we all spend examining the corpse. Theological students are a pampered breed. Pastoral carers by the score waiting to soothe every little ache, ready to pounce on the slightest discomfort.

The assessment process does demand an immense amount of time from all involved. It takes the staff an average of six hours to prepare and write one student assessment report. A Principal of another Ministerial Training Course, on hearing of the time involvement and effort of Pastoral Tutors, staff and Assessors, described it as an invaluable 'love gift'.

The Aston Training Scheme is about vocational development. That will, for some, issue in a renewed lay vocation rather than an ordained or specific full time lay vocation with which they start Aston. Some decide this for themselves, and this may be at any stage of the course. Some, however, have to face an Assessors' recommendation not to continue training for ordained ministry, when their own assessment is that they want to continue such training. Many ACCM Selection Conference candidates have to face up to that, but it can be doubly hard after two years of rigorous training in a closely knit fellowship of ordinands. There is no easy way to come to terms with this. One who went on to train as a teacher reflects two and a half years later as follows:

> When I first heard the news I was naturally very devastated and felt rejected. I had been told repeatedly on Aston that I ought not to undervalue my own self-worth and that I was a 'significant' person. Yet I felt the decision was like a kick in the teeth—it completely undermined all they had said.

Eventually, after prayer and consultation, I decided to accept the decision and that it was God's will for the time being. I still look back now with a certain amount of regret. The reason I was given for being put on the scheme was not to prove myself academically but to gain in self-confidence, particularly with other people. I'm sad to say that the scheme could have done a lot more to help me in that direction. I'm also saddened by the bias which I felt was against an evangelical standpoint.

I do sometimes wonder whether teaching is right for me and therefore whether the right advice was given to me on Aston or whether I should have carried on training as an accountant. I'm sure and have sufficient faith that God knows where he is leading me and that my past experiences are not wasted. I do believe that I shall see much clearer as time goes on.

The Assessors' Viewpoint

The retiring chairman of the team of Assessors after six years is the Rt Revd David Tustin, and he writes this about the panel of Assessors and the way they function:

Who are the Assessors? The Assessors are appointed by the ACCM Candidates' Committee, generally for a six year period. It is essential that the team includes a balance of male/female, ordained/lay, human relations/church experience and a good cross section of churchmanship. It has also been extremely beneficial to have a racial mix on the team. Experience has shown that it needs a ratio of one Assessor to seven students. Because continuity is important, there is a rolling programme of replacements, and new appointments need to be made eighteen months ahead to allow for induction training.

Induction training normally includes a visit to the Aston Centre to meet staff, participation in a residential event (usually Summer School), and sitting in on an Assessors' case conference. Continuing training takes the form of an annual one-day seminar for Assessors and staff.

An essential feature is the corporate mode in which the Assessors function. Although only one Assessor interviews each student, details of all students are available to all Assessors, who reach their recommendations corporately. Thus they can offer one another mutual casework support/supervision/moderation. This is of great practical importance.

What is the role of the Assessors? At the annual one-day seminar in January 1986 the Assessors arrived at the following description of their role:

(1) To enable the candidate to reflect upon his/her progress.

(2) To monitor his/her development, with special regard to the points indicated in the ACCM Selectors' report in the following areas:
> personal growth and self-understanding;
> academic self-confidence and love of learning;
> understanding of one's relationship to the Church and modern society;
> vocation and spirituality.

(3) To be a mirror of what is presented by:
> the candidate;
> relevant information from a variety of sources;
> the staff.

(4) To encourage the candidate to identify and acknowledge areas which need to be pursued and need attention and/or further understanding and development or growth.

(5) To try to discern sensitive or vulnerable areas.

(6) To assess (in consultation and with the support of other Assessors) the suitability/advisability of the candidate for recommendation to the Bishop for further training or alternatives.

(7) To relate to Aston staff. To 'comment' on the effect of the course content and process on the candidate, i.e. how it is facilitating (or not) the life and development and prospective ministry of the candidate.

How do the Assessors Operate?

(a) Before meeting a new intake of students, the Assessors will have received two documents about each of them: the original ACCM application form completed by each candidate (supplying important personal and biographical information) and his/her ACCM Selectors' report to their sponsoring Bishop (which remains confidential).

(b) During the first residential weekend in October, the first interview is held with each student. Its objectives are to enable the Assessor to form an initial impression of the student, to establish a rapport with him/her, and to begin clarifying where development and progress are particularly expected.

(c) At the end of this event—as with the two subsequent ones—the whole panel of Assessors meets for a discussion about each student. Aston staff are present and may participate in discussion (except when final recommendations are being made).

(d) About seven months later (i.e. about May of Year 1), the Principal writes to each student asking for a self-assessment letter, covering such

headings as: personal faith, sense of vocation, spiritual journey, honest reactions to being in the Aston Training Scheme, study skills, academic progress, work worries, personal hopes and fears, targets for the next twelve months, etc. The student is encouraged to use the Pastoral Tutors' help in finalising this letter, and on receiving it and a report from the Pastoral Tutor, the full time staff write a mid-course report for the Assessors. This report is sent to the student concerned, who is asked to reply saying whether this gives a fair picture and whether any further points need to be raised. This process therefore generates four documents for each student which are then sent to the Assessors in July.

(e) During Summer School, the second interview is held with each student in the light of the documents already mentioned. The Assessor tries to help the student to face whatever picture is emerging, and to check its accuracy. At this stage it is especially important for students to identify and acknowledge clearly which areas need further attention, and reset workable targets for themselves.

(f) Towards the end of Summer School, another Assessors' case conference is held, lasting most of the day, to hear about the second interviews and to share first-hand impressions of the whole student body. The gist of what the Assessors feel about each student is fed back to them by a personal letter from the Principal, who can sound a note of warning, encouragement, etc., as appropriate. This is important, because it still gives the student time in which to make a real difference. In many instances a 'shot across the bows' has had a salutary effect. It also means that someone who is unlikely to be recommended to go to residential training can be forewarned of this likelihood.

(g) After another seven months, the procedure of self-assessment letters and Pastoral Tutor report, followed by a staff report, followed by the student's reply, is repeated. These four further documents are again circulated to the Assessors before the final residential weekend, together with a tally-sheet gathering together all the academic grades and supervisors' comments on sermons and pastoral placements.

(h) After Easter, the Assessors participate in the last residential weekend, during which third interviews are held.

(i) Soon after the final residential weekend, the Assessors meet again for their own two-day residential conference to review the outcome of third interviews and, in an atmosphere of worship and prayerfulness, to reach final recommendations about each student. After the initial phase of this case conference, the Aston staff withdraw and any new Assessors

assume 'observer' rather than 'participant' status. Difficult cases are often pondered overnight. The panel then arrives at final recommendations for each student within the range of options set out below, and this is communicated by an ACCM Secretary to the sponsoring Bishop, who makes the ultimate decision. It is an important feature that the Aston staff have no direct involvement either in the Assessors' recommendation or the Bishop's decision.

(j) The credibility of any assessment scheme must depend on its having real teeth. A small minority of those who complete the Aston Training Scheme are 'not recommended' to proceed with further Theological College training. In addition, a significant minority of students arrive at their own decision not to proceed towards ordination but to rechannel their discipleship in some lay capacity; this is not to be seen as failure. Whilst there are others who drop out of the course, the vast majority do proceed to further theological training. The Assessors' final recommendation falls within the following range of options:

1 To proceed unconditionally to further training, usually residential.
2 To proceed subject to certain conditions, e.g. provision of adequate family finance, review by Candidates' Committee after one year.
3 To postpone residential training until some specific qualification or experience has been gained (though this category is used sparingly in these days of high unemployment).
4 'Not recommended.'

Bishop David Tustin adds the following observations:

Experience has shown that deliberate efforts need to be made to bring the topic of assessment well out into the open. This is now done at each event when the Assessors are present, and students are helped to face the reality of assessment without its becoming an undue threat.

A healthy feature is that all the assessment documents generated during the scheme are 'above the table' as far as the student is concerned, though naturally each student's papers are kept confidential from other students.

After some trial and error in the early days of Aston, I feel that the right balance has now been struck between the Assessors being too remote or too involved. They are not present at every event, but have three individual interviews with each student at intervals of approximately nine months. Change is readily discernible over this interval of time, and is probably more striking than if the interviews were closer together.

The spouses of Aston students are not subject to assessment, and are not present during assessment interviews. However, the student's role as a marriage partner and parent is an important element of the agenda to be explored in the assessment process.

When a student is felt by the Assessors and/or staff to need skilled counselling, this can be arranged through the Aston Training Scheme but the content of such pastoral counselling is in no way reportable within the assessment process. Often the student chooses to share some of the insights gained, but this is his/her own choice. Whatever personal development may result from counselling is generally apparent.

The most remarkable feature of the Aston Training Scheme is the way in which the majority of its students make such enormous strides, often to their own surprise and delight. The element of self-assessment proves to be very challenging at a personal level, and fosters a very high level of integrity and openness which cannot but benefit the individuals concerned as well as their further ministry. The Assessors feel very privileged to observe such a heartening process of change and growth, and to play their small part within it.

Although the work of an Assessor is quite demanding, it is also great fun. There are mountains of paper to read, and dozens of faces to remember. One also has to cope with a degree of isolation induced by the role of Assessor. There are also moments of deep perplexity about hard cases. Yet there are numerous compensations, not least the many friendships made and the great hopefulness one feels for the future of the Church.

Here is a letter from one of the Assessors.

An Assessor Remembers . . .

On 9th May, 1986, I finished seven years of being an Aston Training Scheme Assessor. It seemed an appropriate occasion to reflect on the experience!

TRAVELLING

I first encountered Aston on Leeds Railway Station in December 1978 when Robin Bennett, the first Principal, discussed with me the possibility of becoming an Assessor. Since then I have learnt that Aston has much to do with railway stations, motorways and a staggering range of conference centres! From Bristol to Bognor Regis; from

Harrogate to West Wickham via London Colney; I seem to have travelled many miles to the various weekends and Summer Schools.

ASSESSING

I suppose the role of Assessor might be summarised as follows:

(1) to suggest to those joining the scheme, the areas of personal growth and development which will equip them for their later training and ministry;

(2) to stand alongside them (and never over against them) in their journey of self-discovery, in order to discern more clearly with them whether it is ordained or lay ministry to which God calls;

(3) at the halfway stage to monitor how growth and development are taking place;

(4) to rejoice at all that God the Holy Spirit is able to do through the leadership and ministry of the Aston staff, Pastoral Tutors and home Vicars during these two years.

LEARNING

I have learnt a great deal myself. Until I encountered the Aston Training Scheme, I had always regarded education as something very formal. One of the most enlightening experiences of Aston, for me, has been the discovery that Adult Education takes place best in an informal atmosphere where there are definite structures but also ease of communication between the one teaching and those being taught. To watch people who had no time for the formal education of 'school days' suddenly discovering that they could learn and enjoy learning, has been one of the great excitements of these years.

REFINING

I have also been much humbled by the sheer goodness and faith of so many Aston students. Very often, both before coming on the scheme and during it, there has been a refining process of faith which is not only deeply moving, but also points again and again to what the Lordship of Christ means in a person's life. Via doubt and redundancy, bereavement and illness, the individual pilgrimages of Aston students add richly to the story of Christ's Kingdom of Faith.

BELONGING

This would be incomplete without referring to the deep bond of friendship and fellowship and confidence that has existed amongst the group of Assessors under the chairmanship of Bishop David Tustin of Grimsby. We have been a group that respected each other, enjoyed each other and also cared very, very deeply for those students whose future we were discussing and in whom we have taken a prayerful interest. It is a group to which I feel privileged to have belonged.

Testing and Learning

> *A monkey on a tree hurled a coconut*
> *at the head of a holy man.*
> *The man picked it up, drank the milk,*
> *ate the flesh and made a bowl from the shell.*

Assessment on Aston can feel at times as though you're being bombarded with coconuts — even the recommendation to do 'a thing called Aston' can feel like having a massive and unwelcome coconut thrown at you from on high. The stories of the life journeys of St Peter and St Paul in the New Testament have this same feel to them. They were often stopped in their tracks, often affirmed and often brought face to face with themselves by the living and risen Lord. Assessment can be part of the eternal gracious process of our God, for 'speaking the truth in love, we are to grow up in every way into him who is the head, into Christ' (Ephesians 4.15 RSV). The person who needs to take control of the assessment process is the student, for he or she is the only one who can draw the essential benefit and sustenance of the 'love gift' coconut. Assessors, Pastoral Tutors, staff and Vicars often express the great privilege of walking beside students as they make this journey. A former Pastoral Tutor describes it in these words:

> Of my experience as a Pastoral Tutor, there is little and much that can be said. I, of course, learned more than those assigned to my care. Time and again I felt privileged to be party to struggle and pain as an individual wrestled with the meaning of his call by God. Each time I discussed an assessment, I was aware that I was treading on hallowed ground. God had been there before; I was merely helping to make the footsteps more plain and at each moment I was assessing myself and wishing that I had had similar opportunities when I was preparing for ordination.

Part of the original vision of Aston was to achieve an assessment process that was alongside each student rather than sitting in judgment on them. That vision arises not only from a desire by Assessors to be more human about the process, but also from a theological conviction. God speaks within the lives of all Christians and guides us through our relationships with one another rather than simply through the minds of the wise or those in authority.

Experience has shown that such an assessment process demands rather different roles to be played by Assessors, educational staff and Pastoral Tutors, and some roles are closer to the students than others. Experience has also shown that openness by all involved in the process is essential to creating the warm atmosphere in which people can truly reveal and come to know themselves as fallen yet gloriously created and redeemed children and servants of God. It is also apparent that there is an essential interconnection between student-centred assessment process and learner-centred experiential education. Both in assessment and in learning, Aston offers a vision of a way to develop the calling of every member of the Church.

5
AD-MINISTERING

In any college, administration is important, but the chief means of bringing education to bear on college members is to have them gathered within the buildings of the college. The more the corporate life of relationships can develop within the rooms, halls and chapels, the more teaching and learning can take place. The description of Aston as a college without walls falls into the old trap of describing the new in terms of the old, like calling a motor car a horseless carriage and missing the essential new factor.

When we speak of administering the sacraments we refer to the effective bringing together of the recipient and the gift. As Peter F. Rudge has pointed out (*Ministry and Management*, Tavistock 1968, p.4), there is a close connection between ministry and administration. When the Archbishop was elected to the see of Canterbury, 'the dean called for "hearty prayer for His Grace's long life and happy administration". This prayer was more than a hope that the Archbishop might enjoy his office work: it was a concern for the leadership that the new primate might give to the Church.'

Administry brings together, in the right order and in the right proportion, all the people concerned, together with all the necessary resources for learning to take place. Administry also enables learning to proceed at home. All of this has to be done in a spirit which is conducive to the overall objective of the institution. There must be ways of administering help where and when it is needed, whether for a learning problem, or a personal or family problem. The student lost on his way to Summer School, suddenly redundant at work, having a quarrel with her husband, unable to get books, and in any kind of quandary cannot run to his Tutor's study for help. The Aston administration has to be able to provide the help needed. It is not that Aston students are over-protected. Difficulties should be anticipated by the staff, who should also be available to deal with what cannot be anticipated in any precise detail.

Aston is not a college without walls, any more than the Open University is a university without walls. It is a new kind of educational set-up. It requires a shift of imagination from the college concept. Aston is a network, a scheme of complicated relationships made possible and sustained by an efficient and humanly sensitive administration. The main work is done in the student's home situation when he is separated from other members of the course, though still part of the network of relationships. The centre exists for the sake of the periphery; the Weekends, Summer Schools, Assessment Procedure all happen to support what is going on day by day in the student.

The network includes relationships between:

ACCM, the Governors, the Principal and the staff;

Governors and staff and ancillary staff;

Different members of the staff;

Staff and students, on home visits, letters, telephone, as well as at official gatherings;

Pastoral Tutor and student and student's family;

Student and family with Vicar and local church;

Student and his/her family;

Student and other students in formal and informal meetings;

Staff and students and OU staff;

Staff and students and Bishop and his staff;

Student and employer and fellow employees.

It would be possible to identify many other relationships in the network and all of them depend on the right kind of administration. The Bishops' Inspectors, when they inspected the course in 1985, noticed this and that its effectiveness was due to Bridget Edger. They recognised her as the 'anchor' of the scheme. Much more than a 'secretary', she was deeply committed and attended staff meetings as a full member. When the other full time staff were away, as they were frequently, she 'minded the shop', and her carefully acquired knowledge of the students and their families helped her fulfil a valuable counselling role which was much appreciated. She offered efficient administration with a human heart, which meant she also made a contribution to the 'spirituality' weekends. The Inspectors remarked that the efficient administration was exemplified by the Summer School they attended with its six staff, six Assessors, sixty students, thirty wives and husbands, and forty-six children aged 0 to 16. All was supplied at the right time from detailed documentation for the Inspectors to childminders and fish fingers for the children.

A similar intensity and complexity is required in administering an Aston Weekend attended by students, families, staff, ancillary staff,

Assessors, and a few visiting educationalists or senior clergy; accommodation has to be arranged, everything must happen precisely as required to make maximum use of the time together. All of this depends, of course, on countless letters, telephone calls, journeys and the Aston Correspondence, a newsletter which goes regularly to everyone in the network.

If Aston arises from vision and hope for the future it depends on detailed planning to sustain its effectiveness. As J. Moltmann pointed out (*Hope and Planning*, SCM Press 1971) against a rich theological background, hope and planning need each other. Hope without planning does not make contact with the world, is not incarnate; planning without hope produces a technological nightmare with no sense of direction. Hope and planning are operationalised from the administrative centre which remains constantly womanned. And everyone concerned with the scheme knows the significance of that expression.

Administration, to a large extent, depends on adequate finance. As in other voluntary bodies, and in every church organisation, officers do work which should be done by assistants, people do work which should be done by machines and people are continually bumping into each other because the rooms aren't big enough and there aren't enough of them. They regularly take home work for which there wasn't time in the office. It had been planned, certainly, but then there was that phone call, that discovery of a job only half done, the machine going on the blink, an urgent request for thirty copies of that ten-page paper.

Financial anxiety was a burden on Aston from 1977 to 1983. The Central Board of Finance of the Church of England funded the Principal's salary from June to September 1977; thereafter the whole of the scheme's income was to come through fees. But the fees also had to be paid outwards, chiefly to the Open University. Without help from four charities in particular, the scheme's income would have been seriously inadequate.

These generous helpers were Toc H, who made book grants up to 1983-84; the Yapp Trustees, who redirected their grants previously made to students of Ian Ramsey College, also by way of book grants; the Additional Curates Society, who gave a variety of forms of help, including help to students in financial difficulty, and the full cost of an additional weekend in 1979; and from 1982 to 1985 the Society of the Sacred Mission gave a large special grant to assist students' families to accompany them to Summer School, and to help with the expense of the office move from Spring Hill to Westhill College.

This financial pattern (if continuing substantial uncertainty may be so described) imposed a heavy burden on the scheme. Most of this burden was shouldered by the Principal, who was obliged to exert his considerable powers of persuasion to extract support from voluntary charitable agencies. With the benefit of hindsight, it would appear that the Governors left too much to Robin Bennett to carry. Admittedly, the Governors were aware of the difficulties: in 1981 they declared that 'the Church must be challenged', i.e. to bear the costs of the Aston Scheme. They said the same in 1983, when life was becoming very difficult financially, not least because in that year almost all the voluntary grants stopped, or notice was given that they would stop in the next twelve months.

It was at this point in the Aston Scheme's history that there occurred what can only be called a negative miracle. Aston had very carefully budgeted for a slight increase in the number of students who would be paying study fees to Aston but that year they were overwhelmed by a striking increase in numbers which created their first real surplus. Added to this was the fact that Laurie Green, the new Principal, was keen not to appoint a Vice-Principal until he knew exactly what contribution was needed. So it was that by the end of 1984 there was a surplus of £30,000. The Finance and Grants Committee of ACCM took a kindly view and instead of reducing the annual grant, as they might well have done, believed that the scheme, which was continuing to expand, would benefit from having a capital reserve. The fact is that it took seven years and a professional accident to relieve the Aston Scheme of financial anxiety, an anxiety which had in several years almost overwhelmed those who worked for it. For the first time, in 1984, the Governors were able to plan for adequate staff, decent equipment, and expansion in numbers of students and of full time staff.

It was not only the balance of income and expenditure that caused difficulties. Inevitably, with an honorary treasurer whose role was really that of financial adviser rather than financial executive, there were practical problems in the day to day administration of the scheme's money. Peter Dixon, who gave excellent advice to the Governors, could not possibly, with a full time secular job, cope with the steady and continuous obligations of 'keeping the books'. Eventually this function was firmly placed in the hands of Bridget Edger and the gaps in communication and management were filled in. When Peter Wright succeeded Peter Dixon as honorary treasurer to the scheme in 1985, the advisory function was spelt out clearly by the Governors, and

Bridget Edger's appointment as Administrator clarified her responsibility as financial manager of the scheme. Liaison with the Finance Committee of ACCM continued straightforwardly and without tension.

Unlike the governing bodies of any of the residential Theological Colleges or non-residential courses, the Aston Governors are a subcommittee of the Candidates' Committee of ACCM. It might not have been so. In 1982 there was considerable discussion about the possibility of Aston going independent as part of its consolidation, but the new Chairman, Bishop Donald Tytler, was strongly convinced that Aston's future was best secured in close association with ACCM. The new Principal was also of this opinion and the Governing Body agreed that Aston should remain strongly related to ACCM. Decisively, the Candidates' Committee of ACCM took the same line and plans for the scheme to become an independent charity were dropped.

Bishop Donald had been concerned, on taking over as Chairman, to strengthen the ACCM link and to enhance the Governors' role. This concern was expressed in lengthening the Governors' meetings in order to give adequate time for discussion of matters raised, especially of the Principal's report, so that the Church's representatives, including the two Student Governors, were able to participate fully in making decisions.

In the earlier years of the scheme, the Steering Committee and the Governors had run the risk of being merely support groups for Robin Bennett. Support of the Principal is an important role for the Governing Body, but it needs to be matched by the factor of the accountability of the Principal and staff to the Governors. Laurie Green, as he grew into the post of Principal from the autumn of 1983, has been happy in his relationship with the Governors. He has participated fully in giving the Governors a wealth of information, through a full Principal's report at each meeting, about hopes and fears for the future as well as about facts and figures. Indeed, one of the most notable features of the scheme, as it reaches its tenth year, is the quality of the relationships that have been created between the Governors and the full time staff, and through them to the part time staff and visiting teachers.

The role of the ACCM secretary appointed to service the scheme has developed during the ten years. Huw Thomas, having played a major part in initiating the scheme, handed over after six months to Chris Bedford. Without any great vision for Aston's future and having to cope with a charismatic idiosyncratic Principal, and needing also to allay

Anglo-Catholic fears about the latest trendy-lefty outbreak, Chris facilitated and contained and faithfully served the scheme in its most dangerous period, the first three and a half years.

John Oddy succeeded Chris in 1981 and served for over four years until the end of 1985. He took over the link with ACCM of an operation which had the difficult task of moving from entrepreneurial pyro-technics to creative stability. The relationship between Aston Governors and the candidates and other committees of ACCM needed clarification, for Aston, like other training units, has connections with several sections of ACCM. The servicing of the scheme is only one of a Selection Secretary's tasks, and probably a minor one. John Oddy saw that the flow of information had to be improved: ACCM needed both to 'own' Aston and to give the scheme adequate freedom to develop. John Oddy had to spend many hours of research into the difficult questions of Aston's independence, dependence, or interdependence. This particularly affected the conditions of employment of the teaching and administrative staff. The Central Board of Finance was persuaded to re-adopt responsibility, thus avoiding serious difficulties which had arisen in earlier 'pre-theological' training institutions.

To John Oddy must go much of the credit for the successful transition of Aston from pioneering venture to creative normality. He worked away patiently in London, affectionately and deeply committed to Aston yet able to remain detached and objective for the sake of Aston's good administration. Bright ideas were candidly examined, and, if found wanting in practicality, or carrying the risk of undesirable consequences, were courteously sat upon and squashed. Some of John's own words give an idea of why he laboured to help Aston succeed, another example of the way people get caught up in the scheme.

'Flying into ACCM in 1980 after three years abroad in the international, intercultural scene, I found the Home Church strangely hidebound and insular, unaware apparently that much of the world and the Body of Christ had left it behind (e.g. ecumenically and in matters of women's ministry).

'There was of course much happening and much to learn. Five years in-service training with ACCM was to be very rewarding in spite of the above. It was however Aston that caught my imagination, the part of the central church provision which was engaged long-term with individuals, some of whom were the least likely on paper to become leaders in the Established Church.

'Described as a foundation course, Aston seeks to use the raw material of people given to it, so as to enable those people to achieve lift-off academi-

cally, spiritually, personally and ministerially. It recognises that development already achieved in one or other area of a potential Christian
minister's life may not yet be equally matched by growth in the other areas.
Overall development and integration is looked for. Some have thus been
tempted to think of the scheme as though it were a remedial department
with consequent inferior implications. Such have missed the great creative
drive of the scheme, which gives those who happen to be late starters or in
some way among the disadvantaged the opportunity to develop their considerable latent gifts powerfully, and quite likely to overtake those more
conventionally qualified and trained.

'The essence of Aston's programme, the combining of distance learning
with close support of both the academic and the pastoral kind, has set the
pace for future training patterns in the Church. The combined challenge of
the world of study and multi-tradition Christian fellowship with that of
work in the secular community and the local web of relationships is
particularly valuable. The ministerial candidates, whatever strengths or
weaknesses may have been evident in them beforehand, are almost certain
to emerge much stronger and more integrated and confident from
experiencing Aston.

'Today, however, success is the challenge and the danger! Can the quality
and depth of the work be sustained as ever more candidates are sent to
knock at the door of Aston? If it can be, then there will be new life and hope
in the erstwhile hidebound and insular ranks of the Church of England!'

In terms of the types of management listed by P. F. Rudge (op. cit.,
pp.32-3), we can see that the Aston administration has changed from
Charismatic to a mixture of Human Relations and Systemic. From
being a spontaneous creation using the dynamism of intuition we have
moved to a network of relationships but also to a system like that of a
living organism, adaptive, highly conscious, using expert initiative,
clarifying goals, and monitoring change.

Anyone who thinks they can understand Aston without realising the
heightened importance of Admin is making a mistake. One of the
reasons many Aston students have difficulty coming to terms with
Theological College and the Church in general is that they are meeting
organisations which are predominantly Traditional (maintaining a
tradition) and Classical (running a machine).

6
REFLECTING

'I loved Aston,' said the wife of a former Aston student. 'It helped me understand theology.' She had been able to come with her husband on a number of Weekends and the two Summer Schools, as well as sharing the work at home and some meetings with the Pastoral Tutor. The significance of her remark is that she herself is a graduate in theology. Somehow Aston had enabled her knowledge of theology to come to life. The academic discipline often used by journalists to dismiss an argument as theoretical and without relevance to daily life ('merely theological' or 'merely liturgical') had come home to her.

Another student, reflecting on his time on Aston, said, 'God is in the real and ordinary. Our eyes were opened. People don't usually expect that.' And another, 'It did not click in this way at Theological College. There was more standing back and dealing with life at arm's length. At College we became more dependent because we were being taught. The real theology was done at Aston; responding through your own experience.'

None of those responsible for Aston would wish to use such remarks to beat the Theological Colleges and Courses. Their job differs from ours, with set syllabus, information to be imparted, examinations or essays to be 'passed'. The present writer, as a Bishops' Inspector of Colleges and Courses over a number of years, has formed an admiration of, and affection for, the staff members he has met. However, I suspect that a review of Inspectors' reports, which are very strictly confidential, would show that there is nearly always a reference to the need to develop more experiential methods of learning and for the staff to acquire more skill in supervising reflective learning. The staff of colleges and courses are, for the most part, aware of these needs and may be attempting to change their methods, but the pressure to teach 'this and that' is very great. Experiential education means much more than asking for questions after a lecture.

Neither would any of us wish to argue from selective quotations from former students' letters and remarks that Aston has all the answers. We know of students only too glad to put Aston behind them and forget about it. It was inevitable that a general invitation for comment would produce more material from Aston ethusiasts than from Aston critics. Some will have enjoyed the different ethos and teaching and learning style in college. Nevertheless we believe that we have broken new ground in theological learning and not just provided the next stage of the 'pre-theological training' pioneered by the people remembered in Chapter 2.

We now turn to reflecting on the reasons why what happens on Aston is effective in helping the students (and, incidentally, all others helping with the work) to grow as persons and to engage in the practice of theological reflection. What goes on? How can we understand what happens? We shall also draw on the writings of others who have reflected on the way people learn, particularly at the deeper level. Some of these books are quite weighty even in quotation and the reader impatient with theory may be tempted to skip this whole chapter. This would be a pity, because it is an invitation to the reader to engage in her or his own reflection on what is described in this celebratory book. How do you understand, explain to yourself, what actually happens within the people involved? This is not an aimless occupation. It may help in applying the lessons to other learning situations in the Church and perhaps beyond. What follows is an explanation of what we believe happens, and is an invitation to you, the reader, to come back at us with more adequate understanding so that we can modify our reflections and use the improved model to improve the effectiveness of what we do in future.

On Aston, students and staff, supported by the ancillary staff, bring overlapping visions of what it means to be called to ordained leadership in the Church of England, including what is means to be a Christian in the ordinary everyday world they live in. At the Weekends and Summer Schools the staff plan how to focus attention on one or other aspect of the overlapping visions, to examine it through the students' own experience. This does not mean that no new information is given. More probably, specific and detailed information is given which enlarges the students' knowledge of, for example, suffering, which is the subject of one of the weekends. But the knowledge does not remain theoretical. It is linked affectively with the students' own experience. Staff and students share together how they feel about it, how they make sense of those feelings and of the information they have received. And, most important, in addition to focusing on suffering in general and in each person's own life, attention is paid to suffering on the Aston Course including the present event as it is experienced. Thus the adequacy of each participant's understanding and theological explanation of suffering is exposed to examination. When this exposes and reveals a mismatch between experience and explanation of experience there is what in educational theory is called cognitive dissonance, and in Personal Construct Theory, anxiety. There is an unease, a feeling of discomfort which can reach frightening proportions and force the student back into a defensive position, repeating dogmatic statements which at a deeper level she or he knows to be inadequate. With courage, and encouragement, she or he may move forward into a modified, or even reconstructed, explanation, often with a thrill of venturing into the unknown and in a strange way finding it was known all the time.

For example, if you have always assumed that suffering is a form of punishment for wrongdoing, you may find it disturbing to be challenged by another person whose child is dying of cancer. You can doggedly maintain your previous explanation of why people suffer. You can modify it by saying that some suffering is punishment for wrongdoing but there can be innocent suffering as well. Or you can develop a new, more comprehensive explanation involving corporate responsibility in causing suffering and in trying to relieve it. It may or may not help you to be told at this stage that this is what the Book of Job in the Bible is about, that Jung has written an interesting book about Job, and 'here is the best book on the problem of suffering and evil'. The introduction of new theory is one of the skills of the management of learning attempted by the Aston staff. In either case the new explanation has to be tested out in daily life to see if it is an improvement on the old.

The modification or reconstruction of the vision of a participant (staff and spouses as well as students) does not take place completely on the weekend. It is influenced by study of the Christian tradition, supported by Pastoral Tutor or staff group, expressed and offered in worship, discussed with home clergy and church members, and checked by behaviour and discussion at work. Slowly, or quickly, the renewed vision, or system of belief, emerges and can be checked with the tradition which may well be expressed in the terminology of academic theology. But now academic theology is needed. There is an incentive to find out what has been said, how the Bible is relevant, what other traditions say about this aspect of living and dying, how the renewed explanation fits in with systematic explanations of other aspects of life. Academic theology is needed as one of the disciplines assisting in the individual and corporate explanation of life which is not merely

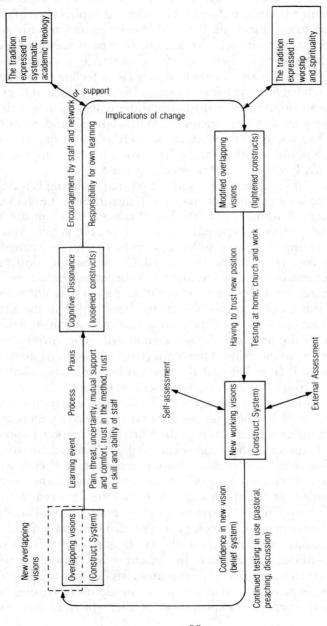

Diagram 4

New overlapping visions

| Overlapping visions | (Construct System) |

The tradition expressed in systematic academic theology

The tradition expressed in worship and spirituality

support

Implications of change

Encouragement by staff and network of support

Responsibility for own learning

Modified overlapping visions (tightened constructs)

Cognitive Dissonance (loosened constructs)

Having to trust new position

Testing at home, church and work

Praxis

Process

Learning event

Pain, threat, uncertainty, mutual support and comfort, trust in the method, trust in skill and ability of staff

Self-assessment

New working visions (Construct System)

External Assessment

Confidence in new vision (belief system)

Continued testing in use (pastoral, preaching, discussion)

The new overlapping visions box is above the old, providing the starting point for a new cycle of creative learning.

theoretical but part of the total way in which the future is anticipated and therefore in some way influenced.

The cycle of learning is summarised in Diagram 4. Starting with the overlapping visions in the top left-hand corner, students and staff move into the learning event of a weekend during which their presuppositions and explanations are challenged within a community which supports the anxiety of cognitive dissonance. Members are not so sure of what they believe but are facing up to more of the experience which their beliefs are about. The support continues when they return home and continue with their studies. Here the Pastoral Tutor has an important contribution in helping the student wrestle with the reformulation of his/her ideas. There is a danger for some students that they will seek refuge in the cleverness of academic theology instead of using it as a discipline to assist in reformulating their attitudes to, and explanation of, the whole of life. They also wrestle with the emerging stage of reality in their prayer and worship. Gradually, or sometimes quickly, the modified or reconstructed vision forms sufficiently for it to be tested at home, at church and at work. Then it can be assessed internally and externally and eventually adopted as the new vision. In the diagram these new overlapping visions are represented by the dotted rectangle, which is meant to be above the previous overlap of visions. Thus the learning cycle is in the form of a rising spiral.

Every such diagram is a gross over-simplification and yet can provide the basis for understanding what is happening so as to enable those responsible for the learning to design the educational process more efficiently and to intervene more sensitively. Every student does not go through each stage: some finish with their vision unchanged, but rather reinforced and affirmed. Some may not be able to cope with the dissonance the first time they meet it and have to turn back — or rather continue round the cycle in a passive way. A risk has to be taken but it must be as accurately calculated a risk as is possible. This is why the Weekends and Summer Schools are prepared for with such care and in such detail.

Such a cycle may be no more than the natural way in which we learn throughout life. At any age we have our own belief system which overlaps closely with others who share our culture, less closely with those of other cultures. It is much more than cognitive, a wonderful mixture from which we may try to sort out genetic factors, conscious and unconscious emotions, cognition, will, faith. It is our own personal working model of the world of our experience, past and present, which we use to anticipate the future, that is, how we view, make assumptions about, meet and interact with, what is happening to us. When our anticipation is realised our inner working model is reinforced and we are encouraged to use it again. When the anticipation is not realised, when things do not work out as we expect, then we can try to explain the discrepancy away, or we can modify our inner working model in the light of its malfunctioning in order that we can trust it again for anticipating whatever the future holds for us.

We see such a process at work in heroic proportions in the Acts of the Apostles. For example, in Acts 10, Peter is hungry, and while food is being prepared for him falls into a trance in which he sees 'something like a large sheet' full of animals which according to all that he takes for granted must not be killed and eaten. Yet he hears a voice say 'Kill and eat.' And again, 'Do not call anything impure that God has made clean.' While he is coping with this challenge to his understanding of ritual impurity the second challenge comes with arrival of the messengers from Cornelius calling him by name and asking him to come with his message to their master. On meeting Cornelius, Peter says, 'You are well aware that it is against our law for a Jew to associate with a Gentile or visit him. But God has shown me I should not call any man impure or unclean. So when I was sent for, I came without raising any objection. May I ask why you sent for me?'

Cornelius describes what has happened to him and how he sent for Peter, and finishes, 'Now we are all here in the presence of God to listen to everything the Lord has commanded you to tell us.' And he waits. It is up to Peter to respond by retreating or advancing. He starts speaking: 'I now realise how true it is that God does not show favouritism but accepts men from every nation who fear him and do what is right.' He continues by giving them 'the message sent to the people of Israel', the primitive apostolic tradition. While he is speaking the Holy Spirit came on all who heard the message, they worship God and Peter says, 'Can anyone keep these people from being baptised with water?' and orders that they be baptised in the name of Jesus Christ.

Peter then has to return to the Church in Jerusalem and somehow involve them in the change which has been forced on him by the events which he now describes. In what must surely be an abridged account of the cognitive dissonance of the Church members, we are told 'When they heard this, they raised no further objections and praised God, saying, "So then, God has even granted the Gentiles repentance unto life."'

Aston students will recognise something of that learning which Peter and the Church in Jerusalem went through. At a weekend the students and staff each bring their own personal vision and understanding of the topic chosen by the staff as most appropriate at that particular stage of the whole course. The vision is part of their understanding, part of the inner working model with which they respond to life. It is the result partly of their own personal history and partly of the influence in them of the Living God whom they have begun to know and whom they believe is calling them to a particular role in the Church as well as to this individual discipleship as Christians. The vision is of them doing something, the calling is to do it and to equip themselves for the doing — the ministry. This idea of ministry is a particular Christian form of what everyone experiences to some extent, the desire for a sense of purpose in life and an active part in furthering that purpose for themselves and, in appropriate manner, for others. Alternatively we can say that the general experience is a partial understanding of, and response to, the call of the Living God. As has been described by Francis Dewar ('Consider Your Call', *Theology*, November 1985) vocation is experienced in two ways, personal and social. In this case the social is within the structures and organisation of a particular branch or manifestation of the Church of Jesus Christ. There is nearly always some tension between the two ways, each being in a creative interaction with the other.

The learning event is carefully planned and makes use of the insights, techniques and theory of adult education. These are based on the empirical study of how adults learn and therefore how the learning can be concentrated. The Church of England has not been backward in recognising the importance of group methods and experiential learning, at least in the Board of Education of General Synod. There is now beginning what promises to be a fruitful interaction of that Board with ACCM (as evidenced in the ACCM Occasional Paper No. 19, *Experience and Authority, Issues Underlying Doing Theology*). The point is made clearly by John M. Hull (*What Prevents Christian Adults from Learning?*, SCM Press 1985) who writes (p.209):

> These considerations [i.e. that the status of learner is not an inferior one, but essential for everyone who is alive, including, perhaps, even God himself] of the place of Jesus Christ in the theology of learning (or unlearning, as the case may be) represents but one example of what might be called the educationalisation of theology which is necessary if the general environment of theological assumptions within which the Christian adult lives is to become more conducive of Christian growth. For approximately two

101

hundred years, roughly coinciding with and related to the rise of modern views of education and the nature of personality, there has been developing an approach to theology which sees faith in educational terms. It is obvious to everyone that the rise of modern science has precipitated a crisis in Christian faith in that scientific knowledge and (more significantly) scientific ways of thinking have challenged the traditional theological knowledge of the world and ways of theological thinking. It is, perhaps, less widely recognised that the rise of modern education has implications for theology and for the life of faith which, although less dramatic than those occasioned by the rise of science, are in some ways more subtle and more deeply penetrating.

The staff of Aston are trained, enthusiastic practitioners of adult education, but also realise that such methods are in fact nearer to those which lie behind what we read of the way the disciples learned from, and in some ways with, Jesus. They lived in a learning community. There was a natural blend of experiential and didactic learning. The parables finished with a question mark, 'what do you make of that?', 'if you have heard, then listen', a kind of invitation to make a break with previously held assumptions and enter the hiatus in which more appropriate assumptions can be formed tentatively and then tried out.[1]

Hence the creation of cognitive dissonance, the loosening of the Construct System of assumptions which had hitherto sufficed. But this has to be planned sensitively, with a knowledge of how much the students (and in a different way, the staff) can take. There has to be the right blend of didactic and experiential learning. These two factors, and other pairs, are not, as is sometimes suggested, mutually exclusive, as if at opposite ends of a single continuum. Rather they are independent or orthogonal and can be represented in Diagrams 5a-d.

In the cycle of creative learning most of the action is in the process of the Weekends and Summer School, with subsequent reflection with the support of central and ancillary staff. But there must be effective contact with the traditions expressed in academic and systematic theology. These disciplines have over the centuries, and in the contemporary situation, taken the experience of people and tested it, criticised it, systematised it in various ways and attempted to make it

---

[1] Cf. Ernst Fuchs, 'Jesus' Understanding of Time', in *Studies of the Historical Jesus*, SCM Press 1964, e.g. p.134: '. . . we may assume in the case of Jesus' own proclamation that he meant to release his learners from every care about the future, in order to lead them anew into this kind of freedom in the present . . . When the parable is seen for what it is, it points the way to a courageous distinction between the present and future, because everything has its own time.'

Diagram 5

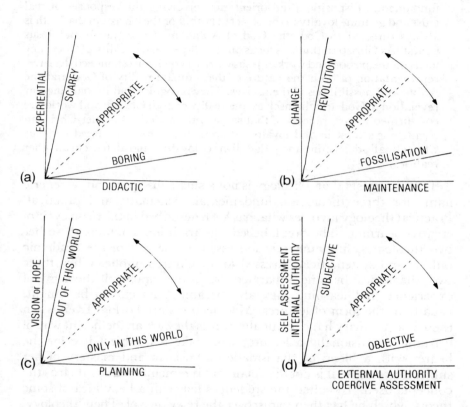

(a)
EXPERIENTIAL
SCAREY
APPROPRIATE
BORING
DIDACTIC

(b)
CHANGE
REVOLUTION
APPROPRIATE
FOSSILISATION
MAINTENANCE

(c)
VISION or HOPE
OUT OF THIS WORLD
APPROPRIATE
ONLY IN THIS WORLD
PLANNING

(d)
SELF ASSESSMENT
INTERNAL AUTHORITY
SUBJECTIVE
APPROPRIATE
OBJECTIVE
EXTERNAL AUTHORITY
COERCIVE ASSESSMENT

Appropriateness depends on area of experience being examined, members of group, availability of resources, ability of staff, time available, support available.

available as a guide to living, understanding and responding to God in service and worship. This development of theology from faith is described by David Tracy (*The Analogical Imagination*, SCM Press 1981, p.47).

> Faith is, above all and prior to any articulation of specific beliefs, a matter of fundamental disposition and orientation involving the responses of real trust and genuine loyalty to the object of faith. For the Christian that faith is always directed to God, the God of Abraham, Isaac, Jacob and Jesus Christ. As Christian thinkers focus on the all-pervasive reality of God, they focus on the person and work of Jesus Christ as their surest, indeed decisive, representation of both the nature of the ultimate reality of God and the reality and possibilities of themselves. They recognise that in that singular revelation of God and themselves, the reality of both Church and world are co-affirmed as real objects of that same faith in God. On inner-Christian terms, one's trust in and loyalty to the reality of God disclosed in Jesus Christ finally determine and judge all other loyalties and all trust in all other realities.

Tracy suggests that Theology is not a single discipline but a generic name for three theologies, fundamental, systematic and practical. Practical theology involves what has been described in the main cycle of creative learning. The box labelled 'the tradition' contains the other two theologies, fundamental, addressed to the rest of the academic public, and systematic, addressed to the Church public. When these two theologies became separated from the practical theology of experience and learning they also became 'subjects' to be taught, usually in the form of lectures. Most lectures are boring. Even when there is a summary handed out afterwards they are an inefficient way of learning. Occasionally a lecturer will make her subject live for the hearer with a blend of charismatic enthusiasm and mastery of her subject. Even then it is not the detail that is remembered so much as the concepts used. Too often the student is left with a hazy idea of some theory which he has then to discover the relevance of. Then 'theology' deserves to become a synonym for irrelevance. When we start with the learning cycle, the need for disciplined thought and systematised experience is urgent and they are drawn into the learning and also modified in some measure by the learning. The student searches for knowledge and the staff should make it available in a form which can be assimilated.

In the terms defined by Tracy, Aston is practical theology, assuming 'praxis as the proper criterion for the meaning and truth of theology, praxis here understood generically as practice informed by and informing, all prior theory in relationship to the legitimate and self-involving concerns of a particular cultural, political, social and pastoral need becoming genuine religious import.'

Tracy continues (p.57): 'Practical theologies will be concerned principally with the ethical stance of responsible commitment to and sometimes even involvement in a situation of praxis. Sometimes, as in appeals to "solidarity", that commitment will be to the goals of a particular movement or group addressing a particular and central issue.' 'They will either assume or argue that the situation is *the* (or at least *a*) major situation demanding theological involvement, commitment and transformation. In terms of truth claims, therefore, involvement in transformation praxis and a theological articulation of what that involvement entails will be assumed or argued as predominant over all theological theories. The notion of truth involved will prove a praxis-determined, transformative one.' Tracy develops this position on pp.69-79.

His conclusion is that practical theology must never be divorced from the other two for its own sake as well as that of the others (p.393); practical theology 'will insist that the transformative power of performative praxis releases the subject to be in the truth by doing the truth'. But without the discipline of academic theology 'the power of transformative praxis can lead practitioners to ever more subtle refusals to engage in critical theological interpretations proper to any theology worthy of its vocation to authentic freedom'.

It was noticeable that Aston students reflecting on their work clearly identified themselves as underprivileged, marginalised, and oppressed by what they experienced as the over-confident and assertive theology of the majority. To some extent 'the power of a liberating praxis' was shared by Aston students, 'the perspective of the outcast, the powerless, the oppressed, the marginalised, all those whose story the rest of us have presumed to tell them' (Tracy, p.398).

The creative learning cycle, as well as describing each learning event, summarises the whole two years on Aston.

The line between the main cycle and the box labelled 'The tradition expressed in worship and spirituality' is also in both directions. Here the collective experience of the Church in liturgy, custom and even style of experimentation interacts with the praxis and the emerging modified or renewed understanding of faith. There is a tension between the two. Similarly the exploration of the student's relationship with God is modified or reinforced. The opportunities to engage in unfamiliar forms of the whole tradition of worship and spirituality are of course greatly increased by the variety of churchmanship among students and staff.

The rest of the cycle follows and leads to a new vision and awareness of vocation which can be brought to the next gathering where over-lapping with others can form the starting point for another cycle. It has been called a 'creative' cycle. We learn about the material world by discovering and uncovering what is there. In addition we learn about the social world by reinventing the way it works in our own system of belief, that is by being socialised. But we learn spiritually, religiously, in relationship with God identified or unidentified, by being reinvented, being recreated, being born again. We find that it is possible to enter a second time into our mother's womb and to be born. Although we are formed by the same succession of relationships and events as before, the effect of them is changed. We reinterpret them. Their meaning and effect on us are no longer as compulsive. They are part of a new way of looking at life. Although nothing is changed, everything is changed because we see it all in a different light. In a sense our experience does change.

There is considerable reference to experience in the Aston Scheme and this book. It is clear that religious experience is not intended. Neither is it the notion of 'a conscious mental going on' quoted by Nicholas Lash (*Theology on the Way to Emmaus*, SCM Press 1986, pp.144f) in order to disagree with it. Rather it is the notion advocated by Lash and based on von Hugel's picture

> of human health and maturity as a function of the continual, practical, costly, precarious quest for the achievement of an appropriate 'balance in tension' between the factors and forces which constitute our experience of the world. In the life of the individual, as of the social group, there is an unceasing struggle between three fundamental forces or impulses: the institutional, the intellectual, the emotional; the traditional, the abstractive, the volitional; the authoritative, the scientific, the ethical...What von Hugel calls the 'three elements of religion' are simply the instances, in the context of religious activity, understanding and organisation, of the factors and forces which constitute *all* human experience.

Other writers can help us towards an understanding of what we mean by experience. George Kelly (*The Psychology of Personal Constructs*, Morton & Co. 1955) was the originator of Personal Construct Theory, which has already been mentioned and of which there is a brief description by Hull (op.cit.,pp.102-13). For Kelly we are all confronted by the flux of raw data, the things that happen to us. These we make sense of by incorporating them into our construct system which we use to anticipate the future. Experience is therefore not so much what happens to us as what we make of it – as if we have a working model of life which enables us to anticipate future raw data as they happen and to make sense of them. The construct system includes all that happens, emotional and personal. We can interact with one another inasmuch as we make similar constructions – that is, have similar experience. Thus the same raw datum could have become different experience for different persons, as most of us are aware.

This way of understanding experience, not so much as what happens to us as what we make of it, is expressed by Rollo May (*Love and Will*, Fontana 1970, pp.225-31). He uses the notion of intentionality to describe the interaction between each of us and the world we live in, between me and my total environment. Starting with a quotation from Aristotle, 'What is given to the eyes is the intention of the soul', May develops the idea of our interaction with the other. We do not passively receive sense data, we appropriate them actively. For May intentionality is 'an epistemology, a way of knowing reality. It carries the meaning of reality as we know it.' 'Each act of consciousness *tends towards* something, is a turning of the person towards something, and has within it, no matter how latent, some push towards a direction for action.'

Aston students are invited to learn within the creative learning cycle, that is to improve their construct system, or their intentionality in interaction with the Christian tradition. It is a change which a Jungian might describe as an improved apperception in which external things are understood more clearly by the registering, responding psyche (Cf. Andrew Samuels *et al*, *A Critical Dictionary of Jungian Analysis*, Routledge & Kegan Paul 1986, p.25).

Lastly, this understanding of experience is used by Paulo Friere, who has been referred to in Chapter 3. A Christian writer, he is quoted by all radical adult educationalists who are strongly influenced by his ideas. Although dealing primarily with literacy he maintains that we became literate by becoming active in shaping our own experience rather than accepting the interpretation fed to us by those who wield power in our society. In other words we take responsibility for what we make of life and we use this experience to change things in the future (Cf. *Pedagogy of the Oppressed*, Penguin 1972).

Most educationalists are aware that as well as teaching subjects or helping learners to explore areas of experience, they are communicating to the learners very clearly through what they do and the way they do it. The learners will learn a great deal about how to teach from the way they are taught. If, at Theological College, the students are put in rows and lectured to or preached at, this is the model they will use with their parishioners when they are set out in front of them. They will try to make their lectures interesting and illustrate their sermons with telling illustrations, but that will not change the assumptions they make about their status as teacher and the parishioners' status as learners. The hidden curriculum of their education will be — you teach the ignorant like this. At least we can hope that for the Aston students who go to such a College there will be an alternative model in their memory of the experience of Aston. We hope that that memory will include the following ingredients gathered from experiencing the hidden curriculum of Aston.

Education is more about what learners do than what teachers do. Learning is a wrestling with experience rather than a passive receiving process.

The skills of learning rather than the skills of teaching are what matter.

Learning is about developing skill, relevant knowledge and attitudes in order to improve and perhaps transform our performance in life.

Most learning takes place without a formal teacher or tutor.

Teachers, trainers, tutors are more appropriately thought of as enablers and facilitators.

It is more appropriate to talk of a learning community than of teachers and students, for everyone has something to learn from each other person and from the interactions within the group. Learning takes place within relationships and those responsible for it are required to participate and give of themselves within the learning community.

Truth is something to be searched for and increasingly committed to rather than something handed down by those who know.

The aim of education is less to do with the absorption of knowledge than with the discovery of the spirit of confidence in your own experiences and learning abilities, and with the gentle humility to remain a lifelong learner.

Lectures and sermons can have their place in these processes as a response to the needs of the exploration. But the method is more likely to be dialogue than monologue.

As John Hull puts it:

The significance of this modern theological development for the reconstruction of healthier attitudes towards teaching and learning in the churches has not yet been widely appreciated. It does, indeed, exist in the churches today, but it exists side by side with [the old didactic methods]. What seems to be taking place is that the assumptions about growth and human personality have profoundly affected the way in which Christian faith is realised, and this is inevitable, because to do otherwise would be to ignore the contemporary understanding of the nature of personhood (op.cit., p.211).

In adult learning, adults are invited to become creative participants in their own development and in the task of understanding and changing the world. We have seen that the very idea of the creation of a free world shows us that creativity is no longer the exclusive domain of the creator. What he creates is creativity. The idea that God himself learns witnesses to the reality, the originality and the creativity of the world, the world of which we adults are part (op.cit., pp.237f).

This chapter is one of reflecting. It is therefore dependent on the activity of Aston, the praxis of staff and students. It would be wrong for the reader to take it as a piece of objective theory to be applied. It can, perhaps, play a part in developing the Aston Scheme and developing the learning process in other parts of the Church and of the world. Which leads to the last chapter which could be called 'Implications' but which we prefer to call 'Dreaming'.

7

DREAMING

The dreaming we are interested in is the kind from which came Martin Luther King's prophetic sermon, 'I have a dream'. Though not at the level he achieved, we can all dream this way and can encourage each other to identify such dreams which carry the implications of our own understanding out into the Church and the world. What dreams do we have – those of us who have been involved in this thing called Aston – about the way it could influence other people and institutions?

Towards the end of the weekend conference of students and staff to help plan this book, we wanted to evoke our dreams for the future of Aston, for Theological Colleges, the Church, etc. One of the staff was asked to lead the session. She started by reading extracts from the popular children's book *The BFG* by Roald Dahl (Puffin 1984).

The Big Friendly Giant collects dreams which he can blow into the ears of sleeping people.

'Dreams,' he said, 'is very mysterious things. They is floating around in the air like little wispy-misty bubbles. And all the time they is searching for sleeping people's ears.'

Taking Sophie, the little heroine of the book, he travels to dream land to catch dreams with his big net and tip them into bottles which he later labels and puts in an enormous store-room. He tries to explain to Sophie that all dreams have a special music which only his 'enormous truck-wheel' ears can hear. In his idiosyncratic English he says,

'Human beans is having their own music, right or left?'

'Right,' Sophie said. 'Lots of music.'

'And sometimes human beans is very overcome when they is hearing wondrous music. They is getting shivers down their spindels. Right or left?'

'Right,' said Sophie.

'So the music is saying something to them. It is sending a message. I do not think the human beans is knowing what that message is, but they is loving it just the same.'

'That's about right,' Sophie said.

The BFG not only hears them, but understands them. He not only stores them but can mix them like ingredients in a cake to produce any dream he wants to blow into someone's ear. 'Dreams *like* being mixed,' he explains. 'They is getting very lonesome all by themselves in those glassy bottles.'

Sitting informally in the lounge at our conference we were asked to catch our own dreams and then, when we were ready, to go and put them into the appropriate bottle for mixing. On the walls were sheets of poster paper on each of which was the outline of a large bottle. Some were labelled and others waited for the labels we wished to give them. We were asked to be quiet for about half an hour, to catch our dreams and, as we caught them, to go and write them in the appropriate bottle. The mixture of dreams in each bottle was then explained and discussed for the rest of the session, thus identifying our overlapping visions for the various recipients, resulting from our various experiences of Aston. Nobody was embarrassed; all were used to working in this imaginative, half playful and yet completely serious way. The ideas formed and clarified. What follows is an edited and expanded version of them, filtered through the understanding and experience of the present writer.

The Aston Training Scheme

It is important that Aston should continue to develop its own way, working from within students rather than trying to impose knowledge on them, attempting to speak the truth in love, continually assessing its own effectiveness and always willing to learn from its mistakes as well as its successes. But it must not become smug and ignore the rest of the Church. Certainly students could be better prepared for the changes they will find when they go to Theological College. Even if the Colleges change, as some critics suggest they should, there will always be a difference of emphasis and students should appreciate the reason for this. They should also be given more help in coping with the Church as it is, with all its human failings, while sustaining the contribution which Aston has made to the vision of what it can become. Then they will be able to give a much more understanding and encouraging lead to the lay people among whom they will minister, identifying and affirming what God is already doing in them. They will realise how difficult it is to change entrenched and unreflective attitudes. They will be able to set about doing what many of them say they dream of doing: sharing Aston with their local Church.

'My home congregation has supported me while I've been on Aston. Now I want to involve them in what I am doing. I'd like to bring the whole Church on Aston.'

Aston must not be tied down in its present form. Lifelong learning means constant change; even the decision to continue doing something as it is must be the result of a review which has considered the desirability of change and decided against it for positive reasons. If it ever stops changing in this way it will no longer be exemplifying what it claims to be teaching, the way to think and act theologically. However, with all the emphasis on the process of learning through praxis it must not lose sight of the importance of a balancing systematic presentation of the Christian tradition which has been subjected to academic critical examination. That branch line from the creative learning cycle to academic theology must be kept open for traffic in both directions and students should be encouraged to see its importance. (See Diagram 4, p.98.) In a very understandable reaction to an excessive deference to the theoretician rather than the practitioner it is all too easy to neglect this essential critical contribution. Once again it is emphasised that the branch line is open in both directions. So too is the branch line to the traditions of liturgy and spirituality.

Many academic and practical disciplines in secular life are relevant to what happens on Aston. Some of these lessons have already been learned through the goodwill of their practitioners, particularly from Open University staff. Other courses, vocational in the secular sense of training students to earn a living, sometimes use methods similar to those of Aston. Certainly other academic disciplines are relevant. It would be helpful to organise a symposium of well-wishers from these other disciplines and courses. They would be told what Aston is doing and asked what suggestions they would make from their own experience and understanding. Those who study language, symbols, communications, organisation, administration, reader response theory, hermeneutics, various psychologies including depth psychologies, those who design learning games and computer simulations for medical and other students — the list is almost as long as a list of human knowledge and should certainly include poetry and art. At least Aston should make a beginning, even though there will not be enough money for the full dream to come true.

There is talk today of the importance of Research and Development in industry. It is no less important for Aston, though almost totally neglected as by all church organisations. Aston should find out much more about how people learn theologically. How does the faith of Aston students grow? Does it move through the developmental stages posited by James W. Fowler (*Stages of Faith*, Harper and Row 1981)? If so, how can people be assisted to move from one stage to the next without losing what has gone before? Are there different types of learning suited to different types of people, as suggested by I. Meyers-Briggs (*Gifts Differing*, Consulting Psychologists' Press 1980)? Aston is in an excellent position to provide the data for careful research. Staff and students (and Governors) are highly motivated and sympathetic to the explorative approach which is necessary for research. Much more needs to be discovered about reflective learning in the field of religious belief, and particularly how it can best be supervised. Could the work on reflective learning in other areas which has been done by the Centre for the Study of Human Learning in Brunel University be adapted for theology? Questions and possibilities multiply. As well as improving the work of Aston itself, such research could be of value to the whole Church.

Psychological testing should be used, direct or in modified form, to monitor change and hence provide opportunity for more informed choice in development, as it is in some Colleges of Education. Computer-assisted learning can also become an aid to reflection useful on Aston. It has already been used in small measure elsewhere and could be tried out on Aston. Aston needs such aids to learning and is not as threatened by them as other sections of the Church. But the Church is unlikely to provide enough money. Is there no charity whose trustees will back the initiative of Aston in Research and Development?

Aston provides a model for collaborative leadership in both the spiritual and organisational areas of Church life. One of the dream ingredients is that Aston becomes unnecessary. It could cease to exist because the Church stamps it out as a subversive movement, though all Christian education is to some extent subversive. It could become unnecessary because the work it does and the way it does it have been assimilated into all the agencies of education and learning in the Church.

Theological Colleges

The aim and objectives of Theological Colleges are not clear. Are they to prepare people for the practice of Christian ministry or to provide the grounding in academic theology which is thought to be necessary for that ministry? If the former, then all too often Colleges are institutional concentrations of inexperience. If the latter, then the work might be better done in a university department of theology. The quandary is the basis of much discussion and enquiry at the present time, together with anxiety over the rising cost of preparation for ordination. The existence of Aston and what it is doing make a contribution towards this debate, which is likely to intensify over the next few years.

Aston demonstrates the great advantages of adopting the methods of secular adult education and implementing them vigorously, including staff behaviour and student involvement in planning. This is not because Aston has climbed on to the adult education bandwagon but because the methods are closer to those of Jesus and of religious learning than are those of the lecture used in most Colleges. Even some part time Courses pump out lectures to tired but colluding students who have driven as much as forty miles after a full day's work for an evening of learning.

The need for change has been clearly stated in some of the Occasional Papers published by ACCM. In the 1982 Paper No. 11 *Learning and Teaching in Theological Education* the debate between adult education and theological training is outlined. 'If either lay people or clergy are to share their understanding with others they need to have thought *how* people learn, and not only *what* they might learn.' 'Perhaps what is needed is some form of "supervision" to help people to reinforce the experience [of the process by which they learn] so that there would be less likelihood of reverting to an earlier dominant mode of teaching when the support of the educational institution is withdrawn.'

Such arguments were taken further a year later in Paper No. 15 *An Integrating Theology* with the call for 'a theological education in the Church of England which would hold together in a creative relationship the formation of a person's own ministerial vocation and character, the acquisition of an appropriate and serviceable knowledge of the living Christian tradition, and an understanding of the forces operating in the contemporary culture both at the individual and at the social level.'

The advice is good. But Theological Colleges and Courses on the whole do not know how to do what is described. Aston has started doing it. It is working. Can such methods be adapted for Theological Colleges? Some doubt if new cloth should be used to patch old garments. Aston was lucky in being able to start afresh.

There have been some changes, as described, for example, by Professor A. O. Dyson in his paper 'Theology and the Educational Principles in Ministerial Training: Problems of Collection Codes and

Integrated Codes' referred to and quoted in ACCM Occasional Paper No. 19 *Experience and Authority*. He concludes, 'A century or more in the Church of England of strenuous and often skilled juggling with the focus and contribution of university and Theological College to the formation for ordained ministry has not produced so far a clear grasp and an intelligible expression of a "more excellent way".'

Aston is a step along the way. The Colleges and Courses have to go further. The Aston experience and fellowship should be an encourage-ment as well as an example of method as they move forward towards new patterns of education to facilitate learning. It is not so much what Aston does that is important, as the way it works as a living organism in which the experience, skills, collaboration, vulnerability, adventure-someness and sense of humour of the staff group provide the nerve centre. It is this blend of attitudes, organisation and personal relations which probably determines the hidden curriculum for the learners. It is sometimes said that it is possible to tell which College a priest went to from his manner and style of ministry. May the manner and style be those of a lifelong learner growing towards 'the whole measure of the fulness of Christ'.

Colleges and Courses work in a competitive style rather than a collaborative one — another ingredient of the hidden curriculum. If they could suspend their autonomy and tradition of churchmanship sufficiently to co-operate in gathering and sharing their experience (including failure) and expertise, in pooling their resources and their 'dreams' for the effective preparation of men and women for ordination, they might be able to move forward towards experiments for some kind of regional resource centres. In these there could develop the creative learning cycle of experiential learning through praxis meeting up with systematic theology and genuine worship. The whole Church of England might benefit not only from the clergy whose formation takes place there but from the kind of lay learning which could also be provided for.

The Church of England

The model of the Church which is implicit in Aston is that of a network of people held together in relationship and administration. The network is not so much that of a fishing net as of the molecular structure of a crystal, or, since it is alive, that of protoplasm or the cellular structure of an organism. It is even more wonderful than that. Members of Aston are usually dispersed in their homes, work places, leisure activities and local churches; yet they are aware of being Aston. They are normally in such a loose relationship with one another that the network is latent. The relationships are available to be activated, and because of this can be relied upon even when latent. Once activated the relationships become operative and the Aston church gathers to share an event of worship, fellowship and learning which can sometimes be like rebirth, being raised to another stage in God's process of redemption and sanctification for some of those present. The gathered event is too intense an experience to be sustained for long, nor is it the main focus of Christian activity which must always be in the world of everyday life. Then, dispersed once more, the Aston church is active like yeast in that everyday life, co-operating with God in the transformation which is his mission and ministry. The two activities, gathering and dispersing, are both necessary and interact with each other.

A member of the Aston church is also a member of her or his parish church. Membership of the one does not preclude membership of the other. This suggests that the Church is a more intricate organism than the parochial set-up we take for granted. People can also belong to other groupings or networks which are latent for much of the time but which can be activated and gathered for a particular church event. A Polytechnic lecturer would belong to her parish church and also to the network church of Poly lecturers and perhaps also to one concerned with her own academic discipline, say Law. The network is concerned with a sector ministry and may or may not be served by a non-stipendiary minister. The network churches might not gather very often. They would remain latent most of the time but there would be fellowship within the latency. When they gathered it would be like true friends who meet occasionally and find continuity. In this way a more intricate model of the Church would be able to serve the intricate world of modern life. Of course the network church must remain in harmony with the main body and not set up in opposition though there is probably a place for creative tension as there is between Religious Communities and the rest of the Church.

Many of the points made about Theological Colleges apply to the Church and to church leaders. Could there not be much more affirmation of the rich gifts and insights of lay people expressed in their own language? Could not a better way be found of dealing with the many reports of working parties and commissions, than by trying to get them discussed by people who have not participated in any way in the process of their production? Much of the discussion at deanery synod level is by people who have not even seen the report. How can they participate?

Two other dreams arise: about self-assessment and about administering. Self-assessment is very similar to self-examination in the traditional discipline of self-examination, sorrow, forgiveness, penance, amendment and joy. Renewed interest in spiritual direction or counselling for individuals and 'Mission Audit' for local Churches and Church organisations emphasises the importance of the thoroughness and openness of the Aston system of self-assessment.

Administering too is important. Too many clergy look down on 'admin' instead of developing skill and the necessary equipment in order to 'get their act together', as one thoughtful lay person remarked. Of course it need not be done by the clergy, but they have the responsibility for seeing that it happens in the right way and in the right spirit.

Those Outside the Church

God does not leave himself without witness at any time. There is a treasure within everybody. The important thing is not that people should get pushed inside the Church but that they should find their treasure, their sense of purpose and desire to minister in their own way to the truth as they see it, and to their neighbour as their self. This, surely, is the way we all begin. Surely the right approach, in the light of the Aston methodology, would be to affirm the treasure as it is perceived and to question its effectiveness. Then it could be compared to the treasure as it is perceived within various traditions of religion. The creative learning cycle would be effective in a much broader way than is necessary for those who already belong to the Christian tradition. Christians believe that it would lead to the Christian tradition as the most effective and most inwardly satisfying — but this would have to be achieved in praxis. Christians who enter into dialogue with non-Christians will experience the vulnerability of genuine dialogue in a very similar way to Aston students and staff within the more limited dialogue of Weekend and Summer School. They can also experience, surely, the creativity of the process.

The Oppressed and the Oppressors

Those on Aston are clear in their awareness of feeling marginalised, oppressed, second class. It is no less a genuine experience for being so much less in intensity than the oppression of the poor, the black, the ostracised in our society and the rest of the world. But it does give a fellow feeling. Although Aston tries hard to accept everyone, it is still possible, and perhaps inevitable, that women and particularly a black woman should feel intensely their second-class status even on the Course. And even when they are integrated into the Course together with their suffering and anger they still have the wider Church to cope with.

Such integration as has been achieved means that the rest of the Course members recognise their own inevitable involvement as the cause of the problem. This is an important lesson, to recognise yourself as oppressed by the Church and oppressing a minority of people on the Course. It is a more difficult task for the oppressor to recognise the way in which he or she is dehumanised. So the women and the blacks on Aston feel intensely the need for all Christianity to be liberating. The rest, halfway between oppressed and oppressor, are able to experience the situation from both positions.

Linking this awareness to the theory of Paolo Freire, we can say that the great problem for most people in our society is that they think they are literate because they can read and write. They are not literate in the way Freire means because their 'literacy' is not linked with praxis. Changing the metaphor, we can say that they are the blind leading the blind. Once they can see, they can speak. The oppressors need liberating as much as the oppressed.

Urban Priority Areas

Faith in the City several times mentions Aston as providing the right kind of theological learning. The staff expected that someone would take this up and ask about the way things are done. No enquiry has been received in the year that has passed since publication. The staff and students, and the present writer, feel that they are not being listened to by the Church. There will shortly be published an enquiry into the Theological Colleges, yet the Aston experience is not included. Therefore the staff join the present writer in finishing this book with an edited and updated version of the submission which was made in March 1985 to the Archbishop's Commission on Urban Priority Areas. We do not pretend that our programme is ideal, but it has at least proved itself operable whilst remaining true to our *vision of collaborative ministry and well-earthed theology*.

What We Have Learnt

A LISTENING AND LEARNING

1 Our students come with an extraordinary richness and diversity of
gifts derived from their past experience, in which so-called weaknesses
can be as important as strengths, so-called failures as important as
successes. Time has to be taken carefully to affirm and reflect upon
these gifts, and the course programme has to be extremely flexible in
order that they are written into each student's Aston agenda.

It would be easier but disastrous to ignore what students come with
and, if we practised such an evasion, they would probably collude in it,
for we note an extreme lack of self-confidence and a weak self-image in
most of them. Most at some time or another have been told that their
gifts are irrelevant to the task of theology and have been frightened by
the mystique with which scholars like to surround themselves. They
therefore think themselves totally inadequate as they are, and initially,
at any rate, beg for the theological data or information which they
believe will make them practitioners of the art of theology.

2 Once this mystique has been dispelled, many of our erstwhile 'backward' candidates prove to be very able students, particularly skilled in
making the faith/life connections so basic to the real theological task.
One of our greatest fears in this connection is that our students, in order
to make up for this lack of self-confidence, will opt for an elitist approach
to ordained or accredited lay ministry. When they are engaged on
church matters students seem to assume the airs of a culture other than
that of their own homes.

This lack of self-confidence is all the more reinforced by those within
the Church who openly look down upon Aston students (or ex-Aston
students now at Colleges) as being second-class ordinands. Our students
then have to cope with their own anger and frustration at being thus
labelled. Some will be patronised at College as the token working-class
student whilst others may find it easier to conform to the image other
students espouse. These pressures are multiplied for those of our
students who are women and/or black, for then it is even more difficult
to hide one's distinctiveness.

3 In order that our Aston students do not defend themselves from these
pressures by rejecting whole parts of themselves (especially their roots)
there has to be positive discrimination to enable those less powerful to
hold their own with the powerful. If there had been no provision such as

119

Aston, many of our ex-students tell us, they would never have survived emotionally or spiritually at College or Course. Aston therefore has at times the feel of the disadvantaged—so akin to the UPA experience. But we find that it is precisely here that theology begins. Aston has by its very nature to address the issues of powerlessness, class, race, gender, etc., not simply as objective 'problems' but as felt experience. This adds to the pain of the exercise, but proves powerfully productive. The Church has much to learn from its 'underprivileged' groups.

B THE LESSONS OF ADULT EDUCATION

1 The focus upon issues rather than a pre-set syllabus forces us to look at our educational models. Remembering that our students, especially those from UPA, have been largely disabled by society's educational structure, the school model of didactic instruction to receptive pupils is largely irrelevant to our needs. The traditional university model of theological education as a learning of the pure truths which must later be applied in practice, ignores what we know about the dynamics of subject and object, misunderstands the reality of incarnation and contextuality, and patronises students who already have experience which the 'teacher' cannot have. Moreover it does not present the students with the tools for doing theology in ministry. As soon as adult educational processes are adopted the course is able to embrace a much wider range of participant, so that not only do our own students feel less intimidated but their spouses and families find themselves playing a substantial role in the whole training process.

2 We have learnt that theological education affects the whole person. It is not possible to confine course work to the academic, for this in turn affects personal development and self-understanding, which in turn affect our appreciation of our roots and our place in society and God's Church. This in turn affects our appreciation of God's call to offer all this in our vocation, which affects in turn our academic perceptions. So continues the dynamic interplay of all these various elements. Our scheme must therefore offer time and place for all these elements to be addressed. For any progress to be made requires at least a two-year period of intensively supported self-searching and mutual assessment. Families must be involved, as must any others who are of special significance to the student. For those students who find in-depth reflection or the development of leadership skills rather alien to them, it is even more important that the learning be carefully integrated and

that they are not uprooted unnecessarily from their formative environment.

3 For this proper integration to be experienced, the place, nature and role of academic study must be properly understood. The students must not be overwhelmed by academia or become its vassals. We therefore offer courses which concentrate on a study of the nature and role of the academic disciplines (the humanities and social sciences) and then integrate the several disciplines thus examined around a theme — such as 'industrial society', 'vandalism' or 'ministry'. This helps students to get the academic task itself into perspective while at the same time learning how to learn. After this they move on to the study of a theme pertinent to their own particular experience. Rather than reading any academic theology at this stage, therefore, we are concentrating on the development of the basic skills required for doing theology and offering flexible models of how the critical and integrating processes of theology can take place. When they eventually move on to Theological College we hope they will know what they want from within the world of theological scholarship, not being intimidated by it, but seeing it as an enhancement of their theological and ministerial resources.

C SUPPORT STRUCTURES AND CO-OPERATION THEOLOGY

1 During the two-year Aston experience students undergo remarkable development and strengthening but also experience tremendous pressures and strains. We are asking them to address the many issues that are coming at them from work (or unemployment), from family, parish, new academic studies, new discoveries about their own person and their societal roots. The ATS cannot expect such pressures to be beneficial unless proper support structures are carefully built in for each student and very precisely monitored. There is an absolute necessity for sensitive pastoral care and oversight of the highest quality. We leave them in close proximity to their roots and ask them to continue using their skills in their place of work, etc., and to reflect upon that experience *in situ*. We are aware that this creates pressure but it can also provide a resource of fellowship and security in that the student will not have been taken away from natural support structures and from an environment that he or she is accustomed to. Surrounding that, we provide academic support tutors, seminars and project consultants, Pastoral Tutors and local lay support teams. We expend much effort in building the Aston fellowship and in addition the students organise

themselves nationally and regionally. The degree of pressure that any student is under must be very carefully monitored. Too little could allow evasion of the issues, too much could damage the person. But in learning to cope with these pressures of living the faith in the urban setting our students are already addressing the problems of urban ministry. They must learn to set priorities, to organise their time, to work efficiently and to find the spiritual and recreational resources to sustain them under such pressure. It is a proper test of vocation and commitment, as there are no institutions to hide behind nor any academic vacations to provide respite.

2 Another important support for each student is his or her own local parish church. It is often the congregation in which the student has grown up and been nurtured in the faith. By maintaining this link we reinforce the idea that ministry is a corporate and not a solitary venture. In the second year, students gather together a local group as part of the research and support for their project work. They value the fact that their training for ordination is thus integrated into the overall training of the whole laity. In turn the spin-offs for the local parish are considerable. Our aim is that the relationship of student, incumbent and congregation should be a mutually supportive and challenging one. We think that most parishes respond well to this endeavour and the student becomes accustomed to a leadership style which is not patronising nor imperialist (i.e. the student is discouraged from adopting the style of leadership which comes in from outside, bringing a foreign, dominating culture).

D REALISING POTENTIAL

Of great importance in the whole ATS operation is the openness and integrity of our self-assessment procedures. These operate as essential elements of our adult education process. We aim to have all assessment and self-assessment on the table, and there is an openness, depth and honesty about it which in some quarters would appear alarming. All aspects of development are mutually evaluated throughout the course and these assessments are fully written up at the end of the year. This means that our students know where they stand and do not assume that issues can be evaded or that ordination can be the only right response to vocation. There is an up-frontness which naturally appeals to many of our UPA students and which guarantees that 'teacher' is not keeping secrets from 'pupils'.

The openness of the evaluations also offers all participants real scope and opportunity for growth and development of potential. Students begin to see this assessment process as part of the theological exercise which they should carry with them as they move into ministry. It is due in no small measure to the thoroughness of the self-assessment procedures that so much potential is realised in our students over the two years. Aston seems to indicate therefore that, given the right environment, student potential can be developed to a much higher level than the Church expects. It is difficult, we know, to select for potential when the candidate has no previous record, but perhaps the Church needs to be prepared to invest in this risk. DDOs, DLMAs and Selectors must find it particularly hard to sense potential in candidates who originate from UPAs. Our experience indicates that the investment of resources pays dividends. In any case, little is lost if it is always made clear to a student that a recommendation is not a recommendation for ordination (assuming of course the candidate is not withdrawn from his or her locality, home and employment). In some cases a Selection Conference recommends that a candidate merely waits for a year or two before going on to College in order that some maturing and development shall take place. In view of our experience that would seem rather an inefficient use of resources and time, for much more could be achieved in those years if the candidate were preparing for College in a more disciplined manner. Potential needs drawing out, and this can be done to great effect.

E BROADENING THE PICTURE

Within the Aston fellowship there is a mixing of different churchmanships, academic abilities, life experiences and personal characteristics. North meets South, UPA meets comfortable middle and working class. Within the friendship which develops, partly in a felt common adversity, these differences are explained and usually appreciated. This is of particular importance to UPA students as their contribution as UP can so easily be missed to everyone's impoverishment. As students reflect on the inter-relationship between the areas and cultures from which they come, they begin to understand the nature and causes of the UPAs and find themselves better prepared to tackle the issues. Students from other areas have their horizons broadened and begin to appreciate the importance of facing the UPA issues back in their own communities even though, in the past, some may have perceived those issues as having nothing to do with their suburban or rural experience.

APPENDIX 1

Sponsoring Dioceses of accepted candidates 1977-86 on entry to Aston Training Scheme:

Bath & Wells	1	Manchester	12
Birmingham	14	Newcastle	5
Blackburn	4	Norwich	8
Bradford	6	Oxford	17
Bristol	8	Peterborough	6
Canterbury	6	Portsmouth	5
Carlisle	3	Ripon	4
Chelmsford	11	Rochester	10
Chester	7	St Albans	5
Chichester	16	St Edmundsbury & Ipswich	3
Coventry	8	Salisbury	13
Derby	5	Sheffield	5
Durham	10	Sodor & Man	
Ely	3	Southwark	9
Exeter	10	Southwell	13
Gloucester	4	Truro	5
Guildford	7	Wakefield	8
Hereford	7	Winchester	9
Leicester	7	Worcester	2
Lichfield	7	York	7
Lincoln	6		
Liverpool	22		
London		HM Forces	2
London *area*	9		
Edmonton	1		
Kensington	10		
Stepney	11		
Willesden	5		

APPENDIX 2

Occupation of students on entry to Aston Training Scheme:

Accountant	6	Driving Instructor	1
Agricultural Research Worker	1	Electrician	5
Bank Employee	2	Engineer	13
Book Binder	1	Environmental Health Officer	2
Bookseller	2	Farm Worker	1
Building Society Manager	1	Fitter	3
Bursar	1	Fireman	1
Buyer	2	Freight Forwarding Manager	1
Carpenter	1	Friar	1
Car Park Attendant	1	Fun Bus Attendant	1
Charity Manager	1	Garage — Owner	2
Member of Christian Group	4	— Manager	1
Clerical Worker	18	— Worker	1
Civil Servant	11	Greengrocer	1
Carpet Cleaner Co. Proprietor	1	Gardener	1
Child Care Assistant	1	Graphic Designer	1
Commercial Assistant	1	Groundsman	1
Chemical Tester	2	Hospital — Ambulance Driver	1
Computer — Engineer	1	— Ward Orderly	1
— Operator	5	— Psychiatric Day Care Officer	1
— Data Processor	1	
— Programmer	2	— Lab. Technician	8
Diplomatic Service	1	Hotel — Receptionist	1
Day Centre Officer	1	— Management Trainee	1
Dairy Herdsman	2	— Caterer	5
Draughtsman	5	— Chef	1
Driver	1	— Owner	2
Dental Technician	1	Health Service Administrator	1
Dyeing Technician	2	Housewife	1

House Person	1	Postman	3
Home Help	2	Pastoral Assistant	7
Horticulturist	1	Press Officer	1
Hospice Worker	2	Quality Assurance Engineer	1
Insurance — Claims Clerk	2	Railway Man	1
— Claims Adjuster	1	Salesman	9
— Manager	3	Self-Employed — Jeweller	1
— Underwriter	2	— TV Engineer	1
— Life Assurance		— Plumber	1
Trainee	2	— Builder	1
— Representative	1	Assistant Scientific Officer	1
Internal Audit Assessor	1	Social Worker	2
Instrument Technician	1	Assistant Social Worker	2
Joiner	1	Residential Social Worker	1
Land Agent	1	Secretary	1
Library Clerk	1	Student	18
Local Government Officer	11	Security Officer	1
Manager	9	Stage Crew	1
Assistant Manager	4	Services — Royal Navy	1
Magisterial Officer	1	— Merchant Navy	2
Milkman	1	— Army	1
Miner	1	Specifications Assistant	1
Meter Tester	1	Train Traffic Control Assistant	1
Magician (Trainee)	1	Travel Agent	1
Machine Tool Setter	1	Teacher	9
Mission to Seaman Assistant	2	Trust & Tax Assistant	1
Nanny	1	Unemployed	12
Nurse — District	1	Voluntary Worker	7
— Student	2	Verger	2
— RMN	1	Assistant Warden	2
— SEN	4	Welder	1
— SRN	5	Warehouseman	4
— Psychiatric SEN	3	Workstudy Trainee	1
— Auxiliary	4	Youth & Community Worker	13
Personnel Officer	1	YOP Supervisor	1
Policeman	10		
Project Manager	1